CRITICAL RELIGION READER

Edited by Melanie Barbato, Cameron Montgomery and
Rajalakshmi Nadadur Kannan

ISBN: 978-1-7753943-6-5

Copyleft 🄯2020. You may photocopy, scan, print, and otherwise share the contents of this book in whole or in part providing you attribute the work to the authors who wrote it.

Studio Dreamshare Press
Pembroke, Ontario, Canada www.StudioDreamshare.com
Inquiries: studiodreamshare@gmail.com

CONTENTS

PREFACE   1

Timothy Fitzgerald

INTRODUCTION   6

What is Critical Religion and Why Does It Matter?   7
Melanie Barbato, Cameron Montgomery, Rajalakshmi Nadadur Kannan

CRITICAL RELIGION AND THE ARTS   12

Jackie Kay's Encounter With Double-Consciousness and 'Religion'   13
Fiona Darroch
A Profession of Imaging Religion   18
Paige Medlock
Blurring the Boundaries – Punk Rock And Religion   23
Francis Stewart
Logic, Poetry, And The Myth Of Disenchantment   27
Melanie Barbato

CRITICAL RELIGION AND POLITICS   31

"The Discourse on Good and Bad Secularism: A Contemporary Genealogy of Secularism in France."   32
Per-Erik Nilsson
'Religion' and the Study of 'Religious Leadership': Some Observations From Lebanon   38
Alexander Henley
Tibetan Self-Immolation Between Religious Practice And Political Statement   44
Carolina Ivanescu
Critical Politics   48
Timothy Fitzgerald

CRITICAL RELIGION AND ECONOMY — 54

Fictions and Contentions: Critical Religion in a Time of Crisis — 55
Brian Nail
"Profits of Doom" — 62
Andrew W. Hass
Postmodernism, Postcolonialism, and the Private Property Society — 68
Timothy Fitzgerald

CRITICAL RELIGION, GENDER AND SEXUALITY — 71

Critical Religion and Female Genius — 72
Alison Jasper
The Bible and Homosexuality — 75
Alison Jasper
Performing Gender and Sexuality in Early 20th Century India — 80
Rajalakshmi Nadadur Kannan
An Argument For Thinking of Religions as Vestigial States — 85
Naomi Goldenberg
Feminism and Critiquing Categories in Religious Studies — 91
Cameron Montgomery
Gender and Career Progression in Theology and Religious Studies — 96
Katja Neumann

CRITICAL RELIGION AND EDUCATION — 102

The Marketization of the Academy for Profit – Is it Founded on the Myth of Religious Violence? — 103
Francis Stewart
Creativity, Academia and Critical Religion — 107
Michael Marten
What is the University For? — 113
Andrew W. Hass

CRITICAL RELIGION AND NON-WESTERN CONTEXTS   118

The Perry Expedition (1853-1854) and the Japanese Encounter with 'Religion'   119
Mitsutoshi Horii

The Harris Treaty (1858) and the Japanese Encounter with 'Religion'   125
Mitsutoshi Horii

The "No True Scotsman" Fallacy and the Problem of Identity   134
Michael Marten

Postcolonial and Subaltern Rethinking of Critical Religion   140
Rajalakshmi Nadadur Kannan

Words Don't Come Easy: An Example From Jaina Studies   146
Melanie Barbato

Who Defines Religion in the Colony?   150
Alexander Henley

Some (Mainly) Very Appreciative Comments on Brent Nongbri's Before Religion: A History of a Modern Concept   155
Naomi Goldenberg

AUTHOR BIOGRAPHIES   159

PREFACE

In 2018 I contacted three brilliant academics, the editors of this volume, and asked them to select and edit a collection of 1000 word essays that had been published on the **Critical Religion Association (CRA)** website. They had written some of the best of these themselves. (Though this website is strongly associated with the University of Stirling and its Religion subject area, it is in fact off-campus). These three have produced this Reader. I am grateful to these excellent scholars - **Dr Rajalakshmi Nadadur Kannan (Raji), Dr Cameron Montgomery** and **Dr Melanie Barbato** - for finding the time and energy to achieve this, when all three have their own busy academic and personal lives to lead in the precarious conditions of the times.

I want to stress that, though I initiated this Reader, I stayed completely out of the selection and editing process. This was done solely by Raji, Melanie and Cameron. This is their publication.

We all live in different countries and on different continents. I am in Australia; Cameron is in Canada; Melanie is in Germany; and Raji is in Japan. We are all in different time zones. We are all trying to scratch a living in the precarious conditions of global capitalism. And we are all trying to protect ourselves and our loved ones from the global pandemic of covid-19.

I want – briefly - to give a bit of background here so our readers can understand the conditions that gave rise to this volume, and to the Critical Religion Association (CRA) website in the first place. It was our Stirling colleague **Michael Marten** who set up the CRA website. And though several people shared the work of editing, Raji - **Rajalakshmi Nadadur Kannan** - did as much and perhaps more than most to assist Michael. I thought that the ideal person to coordinate the task of compiling and editing this book was Raji. Raji wrote her PhD thesis at Stirling, jointly supervised by myself and Michael (2009-2014). Raji was a major editorial contributor to the critical religion webpage set up by Michael while she was simultaneously researching and writing her PhD, as well as doing teaching and lecturing duties for the religion subject area.

Melanie Barbato was one of our most brilliant undergraduates at the University of Stirling in my memory. She was an outstanding member of an exceptionally talented cohort of students at that time. In addition to her excellent writing and intelligent contributions to our seminars, Melanie was active with other students in helping to organise a series of student group workshops in Critical Religion. Since leaving Stirling she went on to a doctorate in Indology and Religious Studies from LMU Munich, and then to publish her monograph on Jaina philosophy.

Cameron Montgomery's PhD was supervised by Professor **Naomi Goldenberg** at the University of Ottawa. It was therefore by way of Naomi that Cameron became interested in critical religion. Naomi has long been one of the most prominent theorists and activists contributing to critical religion, as well as a good friend to the department at Stirling and to me personally. To have both Naomi and her multi-talented student Cameron contributing to critical religion strengthens the visibility and the plausibility of the enterprise. It was on a visit to Ottawa that I first met Cameron, and we met again later with Naomi on a train journey between Uppsala and Lund in 2014. We had been with 40 or 50 colleagues at the Critical Religion conference at Uppsala, and were on our way to Lund University to give a public lecture there. Cameron has many creative talents in addition to her academic work. It is Cameron's own publishing company **Studio Dreamshare Press** that is producing this Reader.

Critical Religion, understood as *the critical study of 'religion' and related categories,* was adopted early as the symbol and focus for the work of the religion subject area at Stirling University, and this became more visible when Michael joined us at Stirling in 2008 and the establishment of the CRA website. There were four of us full-time in religion by this time – **Alison Jasper, Andrew Hass, Michael** and myself. Michael Marten set up and edited the webpage with imagination and technical skill, as well as carrying the normal heavy teaching load and contributing significantly to the development of our courses. The CRA website replaced an earlier website, the **Critical Religion Category Network (CRCN)**, which I had set up in around 2004 with the help of a visiting American student. This was around the time of the first critical religion conference, "Religion and the Secular: Historical and Colonial Formations", which took place at Stirling in 2003. That conference generated the essays collected in a book edited by myself and published by Equinox in 2007 under the title Religion and the Secular:

Historical and Colonial Formations. However, the smart American student who set it up for me had to return to the USA, and my own lack of skills in using webpage software meant that the CRCN webpage never got much off the ground. When Michael arrived, he improved things greatly with the CRA website. The website is still live - even though Michael, Alison and I have all retired. The current caretaker is **Dr Bashir Saade**, who is lecturer in Religion and Politics at Stirling.

There were many other colleagues, friends and former students who contributed to the religion subject area at Stirling, and I confine myself to those who have contributed essays to this volume, selected by the three editors. **Dr Fiona Darroch, Dr Katja Neumann, Dr Paige Medlock, and Dr Francis Stewart**, all did their PhD's at Stirling, and all contributed greatly to our diverse subject area, as teachers, course developers, essay markers, webpage editors, and as valued colleagues generally. The diversity of their special interests is a good sign of the relevance of critical religion to many different topics.

Three of the contributors to this volume – **Dr Per-Erik Nilsson (Pelle), Dr Mitsutoshi Horii (Mitsu), and Dr Alex Henley**, have made substantial contributions to critical religion. Pelle, Mitsu and Alex are significant theorists in their own right. They all pay close attention to the religion-secular binary operations in distinct and specific contexts: Pelle's work on the controversies over Muslim dress codes in France; Alex's work on Islam in Lebanon; and Mitsu's work on the invention of religion and politics in Japan. They are all concerned with cognitive imperialism and the legacy of colonial and neo-colonial hegemony. They have been regular contributors to critical religion for years, and they have made substantial theoretical contributions in their own publications, and through their presence at critical religion seminars, workshops, and conferences. Alex has also been running a critical religion series of invited guest speakers at Oxford.

Finally I pay tribute to **Dr Brian Nail** and **Dr Carolina Ivanescu**, and express our gratitude to them for their effective contributions. Carolina's work with Tibetan diaspora and refugees and the practice of self-immolation, and Brian's exposure of faith in the myth of self-regulating markets held by the experts who run the Federal Reserve Bank, are very interesting topics in themselves, and act to further destabilise the discourse on religion and religions and their supposed essential difference from secular practices.

On a day to day basis, until the end of 2015, it was Alison, Andrew, Michael and I who formed the core subject area group at Stirling. We took all decisions on a collective, democratic basis. We each had and have our own area of expertise, and we did not necessarily always agree what critical religion is or ought to be. Inter-disciplinarity is not merely close to our heart as a nice sentiment, as Andrew Hass has pointed out in his piece here "What is a University?". Inter-disciplinarity is inescapable for critical religion. The category 'religion' is uncritically reproduced throughout the academy, not only in religious studies. The very idea of a secular university requires the idea of religion by mutual exclusion. Historians, philosophers, anthropologists, and just about everyone else in the Humanities and Social Sciences deploy the term 'religion' as though it is a fixed, unitary sign that refers to some self-evident feature of the world. In this sense it is a transcendental illusion, with its endlessly contested meaning and history concealed beneath an appearance of stability and coherence. But then almost exactly the same can be said about its parasitic other, 'the secular' and 'secularity'. The illusions of secularity and secular reason can only pretend to be independent of the modern discourse on religion. We tried to collaborate as much as we could with colleagues in other subject areas, though this proved to be difficult for all sorts of reasons.

 One thing that united us in our 'critical religion' inflected teaching was our interest in our students, undergraduate as well as graduate. As well as teaching courses that fitted our own expertise, we wrote and taught core undergraduate lecture courses together as teamwork, which worked well. Our students at Stirling seemed on the whole to like them. Our students were always lively, sometimes brilliant people and full of early enthusiasm at the prospect of new knowledge, extended vocabulary, and interesting debates. That is, until the sheer grind of chasing grades got to them, like a continuation of the secondary school obsession with mechanical, robotic learning. We had lots of positive feedback and support from our undergraduates though. We have them to thank for testing us during our lectures and seminars and pushing us towards greater clarity. We hope that this Reader will be useful and perhaps inspire some of them.

 As the *After World Religions* volume edited by David Robertson and Christopher Cotter (Routledge, 2016) powerfully indicates, it is not easy teaching religion while simultaneously historicizing and deconstructing the category 'religion', 'religions' and 'world religions'. It feels counter-intuitive. However, that is a characteristic of critical thinking. It is as though we are exposing one illusory topic 'religion' in order to see the world more clearly, to be more aware of the ways our very general categories tend to reproduce an ideological formation serving specific interests while seeming to be merely descriptive and objective. Furthermore, 'religion' is not a stand-alone category, and, logically, other related categories such as secular, politics, nation state, modern, economics or progress (to give a few examples) require similar historicization. These reified rhetorical categories appear like value-neutral common sense. We use them with automatic but unconscious ease. However, this leads to very complex theoretical and pedagogical issues and for obvious reasons this more extended agenda was not so prominently pursued. The unstable and contested term 'religion' and its parasitic relation to 'non-religious secular' remained as the primary reference point.

Discourses on 'religion' are very much connected to colonial and neo-colonial power relations, and to constructions of 'race' and 'gender'. These have been significant markers of inequality and discrimination, lurking behind pseudo-scientific classifications and the advance of 'knowledge'. These issues of race and gender constructions are integral to critical religion.

The short essays here, which can be read at a sitting on a train or bus journey, or as a quick feed of ideas for further research on some project, are a good way to inform a wider audience about the theoretical and methodological implications of critical religion. I hope that many people, regardless of whether they are undergraduate, postgraduate or faculty, or members of the reading public, and regardless of whether they are in religious studies, political studies, postcolonial studies, economics, history, Eng.Lit, Sports, or any other discipline, will read through this collection, and notice the great range of topics that lend themselves to critical deconstruction of religion and the religion-secular binary. I am grateful to the three editors, my Stirling colleagues, and all the contributors for their originality and creativity in pursuing this critical agenda.

Timothy Fitzgerald

INTRODUCTION

WHAT IS CRITICAL RELIGION AND WHY DOES IT MATTER?

This volume presents 26 short articles that span topics from stained glass to homosexuality to the Research Excellence Framework, and which have geographically diverse foci from Britain to Lebanon to Japan. What brings them together is that they all share a critical approach to the concept 'religion'. The word 'critical' here should be understood in a positive sense: scholars of Critical Religion seek to illuminate the various uses of the category 'religion' and reflect on the consequences that follow from some communities and their practices, texts, behaviours or objects being labelled as either 'religious' or 'non-religious'.

Critical Religion's entry point is the understanding that religion is not a thing that is simply there 'in the world'. While many people would claim that they know a religion 'when they see one', there are ongoing debates in Religious Studies on how to define the very subject of the discipline, or whether it should be defined, or whether in academic discourse we should even have a term 'religion' that is wrought with so many complexities and associations with conflict and violence.

Critical Religion emphasizes that the category religion has developed in a specific historical context. In particular, many of the current connotations of 'religion' have been shaped by enlightenment thinking and the assumption that there should be a private sphere of religion separate from the public sphere of politics. The idea of what 'religion' is was almost exclusively modelled on notions of Christianity and to a lesser degree Judaism and Islam, all monotheistic traditions that share common roots. Hence, when Europeans came into contact with other cultures, some of the practices they encountered were labelled as 'religious' on the basis of how much they resembled what they knew from back home.

Studies of Critical Religion have shown that these categorisations often failed to adequately reflect the cultural context in which they were situated. In particular, scholars of Critical Religion ask critical questions as to who benefits in these contexts from a specific understanding of religion and the construction of dichotomies such as religious/secular, emotional/rational, backward/civilised. For example, if monotheism is presented as the ideal representation of religion, some people or groups may seek to present their own tradition in line with this ideal to avoid being labelled as inferior. Or, if a law grants protection to some form of religion, there may be arguments as to whether a certain practice counts in this context as religion or not, directly linking definitions of religion to the enjoyment of or exclusion from certain privileges. This applies both to the colonial contexts and to contemporary debates on foreign policy, minority rights and civil liberties.

While all scholars of Critical Religion agree that 'religion' is not a straightforward category, they draw different conclusions. Some scholars have concentrated their research on descriptive accounts, some argue that the category religion is so problematic that it should be done away with, and some consider the category religion as useful when it is employed in a reflective manner. Some have taken an explicitly postcolonial or feminist stand that seeks to call out the injustices into which the use of the category religion has been entangled, calling for revised and more inclusive approaches. Scholars of Critical Religion may define themselves as religious or non-religious, or they may reject the category. What this points to is not the absence or the need for cohesion of ideas on religion in academia and in society, and the book will not aim to provide straightforward answers to such questions. Rather, it seeks to support the central task of Critical Religion, which lies exactly in highlighting the problematics that arise from the homogenization of the meaning of 'religion'.

Moreover, this book wants to highlight the diversity of issues to which the approach of Critical Religion can be applied as well as the diversity of voices within Critical Religion. The short texts can be read independently of each other and make ideal reading for the classroom. They are meant not as the finishing line but as a starting point and a guide for discussion.

While the primary readership is envisaged to have some background in Religious Studies, we believe that this book will be of interest to anyone who is interested in critical thinking and the impact that categories and concepts have on our life. For, as Michael Marten pointed out, Critical Religion could really also be called Critical Categories, and the critical thinking skills gained from Critical Religion can and have been applied to an almost infinite number of topics.

All the articles in this reader have been published previously on the blog of the Critical Religion Association. We would like to thank Timothy Fitzgerald for initiating this publication. The articles were originally published between 2012 and 2016, and most of them have undergone minor revisions for republication. While some of the context has naturally shifted since the original publication, the underlying theme of challenging oversimplified dichotomies has remained the same. We therefore believe that these articles have stood the test of time and remain thought-provoking and informative.

For this book, we have selected six key themes, each containing three to seven short texts that throw spotlights on how Critical Religion can be applied to the respective field. The themes are: 1) Critical Religion and the Arts, 2) Critical Religion and Politics, 3) Critical Religion and Economy/Capitalism, 4) Critical Religion, Gender and Sexuality 5) Critical Religion and Education, 6) Speaking of 'Religion' in Non-Western Contexts.

In the section **Critical Religion and the Arts**, the first contribution by Fiona Darroch discusses questions of 'religion' and identity in the writings of the poet and novelist Jackie Kay, who was born to a Scottish mother and Nigerian father. Paige M. Medlock examines the complex meaning of stained glass in religious and secular institutions. Francis Stewart describes how for many of the people she interviewed for her doctoral research, punk rock became a form of "desacralised salvation". Drawing on poetry and Indian logic, Melanie Barbato explores the fluid boundaries between aesthetics, religious belief and rational argumentation.

The section **Critical Religion and Politics** starts with a reflection on Islam and secularism in France by Per-Erik Nilsson. On the basis of his research in Lebanon, Alexander Henley outlines some typical misconceptions about the notion of 'religious leadership'. Carolina Ivanescu discusses the intersection of political and religious goals in Tibetan self-immolation. Timothy Fitzgerald argues that in modern discourse 'religion' often functions as half a binary of 'religion/politics', and that we therefore not only need Critical Religion but also Critical Politics.

In the section on **Critical Religion and Economy/ Capitalism**, Brian Nail discusses the role Critical Religion can play in understanding the economic and environmental crises that have come to define the current age. Andrew Hass then draws on Walter Benjamin to reflect on guilt in the religion of capitalism. The section is rounded off by another contribution by Timothy Fitzgerald, which discusses how the category 'religion' has been used as mythical basis for the private ownership of the earth.

Under the heading of **Critical Religion, Gender and Sexuality**, Alison Jasper makes the case why Critical Religion can be a desirable tool for feminist academics. In a second piece, she tackles the issue of homosexuality in the bible, and argues that the religion/secular dichotomy is unhelpful for understanding contemporary attitudes to homosexuality. Rajalakshmi Nadadur Kannan shows in her contribution that discourses about female sexual propriety were central for the redefinition of performance arts in 20th century India. Naomi Goldenberg suggests thinking of religions as vestigial states as a tool for Critical Religion, which could be particularly useful for analyzing gender in religion and politics. Katja Neumann's examines the reasons for the gender imbalance in Theology and Religious Studies.

This leads over to the next section, **Critical Religion and Education**. Francis Stewart asks if the marketization of the Academy is based on the myth of religious violence. Michael Marten argues that the quantification mechanisms that are used to evaluate academic performance in the UK are unable to do justice to the creative and interdisciplinary work done by scholars engaged in Critical Religion. Andrew Hass calls for a renewed debate on the University's current identity crisis and the ruling paradigms that underlie this crisis.

While the previous contributions have already involved a variety of geographical locations, the final section on **Critical Religion and Non-Western Contexts** specifically discusses the issues that arise from transferring concepts such as the religious/secular dichotomy into non-Western settings. Mitsutoshi Horii first examines the notions of 'politics' and 'religion' in the letters of the Perry expedition (1853–1854). He then discusses the clause on 'religion' in the Treaty of Amity and Commerce that was negotiated by America's first consul to Japan in 1858. Using the No true Scotsman fallacy as a starting point, Michael Marten offers a constructivist approach to Critical Religion to leave behind essentialist notions of what constitutes *true* forms of identity. He addresses not only those who use categories like 'religion' uncritically but also scholars of Critical Religion who hold strong views as to how people in non-Western contexts should use these contested categories.

Focusing on identity construction in 20th century India, Rajalakshmi Nadadur Kannan calls scholars of Critical Religion to take seriously indigenous agency and the variety of ways in which concepts such as science or religion were used by both Indian nationalists and subaltern groups. Melanie Barbato describes the conceptual challenges she faced when seeking to write about the Jaina teaching of anekantavada for a predominantly Western readership. Discussing the proclamation of the new state of Lebanon, the article by Alexander Henley asks who defines religion in the colony. Naomi Goldenberg offers a review of Kent Nongbri's *Before Religion* that discusses how the critical approach of Nongbri's book could be strengthened further.

A note on British vs. American vs. Canadian English spelling conventions: we left it up to the preference of each contributor.

CRITICAL RELIGION AND THE ARTS

JACKIE KAY'S ENCOUNTER WITH DOUBLE-CONSCIOUSNESS AND 'RELIGION'

Fiona Darroch

Jackie Kay was born in Edinburgh in the 1960s to a Nigerian father, and a white mother from the Highlands. She was adopted by a white couple who were active members of the Communist party, and she is a graduate of, and holds an honorary doctorate from, the University of Stirling, Scotland. She is the author of novels such as *The Trumpet*[1] and collections of poetry such as *The Adoption Papers*.[2] She has also published her witty and heartfelt memoirs, *Red Dust Road*,[3] about her upbringing and being reunited with her birth parents. The opening chapter is an amusing account of her first meeting with her birth father in a hotel room in Nigeria, which raises fascinating questions about 'religion', and identity:

> And now we're in the room. I'm about to have a conversation with my birth father for the first time.
> Jonathan is moving about from foot to foot, shifting his weight from side to side, like a man who is about to say something life-changing.

---

[1] Jackie Kay. *The Trumpet* (London: Picador, 1998).
[2] Jackie Kay. *The Adoption Papers* (Northumberland: Bloodaxe Books, 1991).
[3] Jackie Kay. *Red Dust Road* (London: Picador, 2010).

He begins: 'Before we can proceed with this meeting, I would like to pray for you and to welcome you to Nigeria.' I feel alarmed. Extreme religion scares the hell out of me. It seems to me like a kind of madness. But it is obvious to me that Jonathan won't be able to talk at all if I try and skip the sermon, 'OK, then,' and he says, 'Sit, please.' And I sit.

He plucks the Bible from the plastic bag. Then he immediately starts whirling and twirling around the blue hotel room, dancing and clapping his hands above his head, then below his waist, pointing his face up at the ceiling and then down to the floor, singing, 'O, God Almighty, O God Almighty, O God Almighty, we welcome Jackie Kay to Nigeria. Thank you...' He does some fancy footwork. He's incredibly speedy for a man of seventy-three. He's whirling like a dervish.

I shift uneasily in my seat. Christ Almighty, my father is barking mad...

When I tell my mum about it on the phone, down an incredibly clear line from Abuja to Glasgow, how he doesn't want to tell any of his children, and how I must remain a secret, how he feels I am his past sin, she says: 'By God, did we rescue you!'[4]

As an academic in Scotland specialising in critical religion and culture, and in postcolonial literature, what do I do with this extract? As a teacher, and a researcher, here are some of the questions I would start with: How do we make sense of the concept of 'religion' that is portrayed? What does it tell us about national identity, about Scottish identity? What role does humour play? How can this whole extract inform us to think creatively about writing about religion and postcolonial literature? In many ways, the reader is presented with the meeting of European rational thought, and non-western modes of thought. The awkwardness of this incredibly personal moment makes us laugh.

For Jackie Kay this is the meeting with the fabric of herself, her ancestry, and therefore a significant part of her identity, an identity that is also rooted in European and Scottish rational thought, an identity that rests on a safe distance maintained between religious and secular spaces.

The imposition of this almost ecstatic religious display within the confines of a Hilton hotel room leaves Jackie Kay in a state of semi-

---

[4] Kay. *Red Dust Road*, 3-11.

consciousness: "I've zoned out now, drugged by his voice. I go in and out of consciousness like somebody who's very ill. I can't see properly".[5] Kay playfully suggests that she has succumbed to a 'religious' trance and is losing grip on her post-Enlightenment, rational, secular self. I am intrigued by the complexity and contradictions of this exchange; the banal yet often embedded notion of appropriate, so-called 'religious' behaviour or the impact of colonial violence? Are we laughing because we can safely sit in our armchairs *knowing* that we are choosing not to believe, or that we at least know how to contain our religious self appropriately? Or what about what Kay sees, which is the crude imposition of Christianity on African culture leaving behind a ludicrous mimicry and madness. To classify Jonathan's display as a colonial mimicry is to subjugate and 'exoticise' his voice again, but this time by the western (postcolonial) academic. Graham Huggan talks about the risk that the marketing of postcolonial literature takes by 'replicating the exotic consumption of otherness'. Is our laughter merely a crude consumption of this display of 'otherness'?[6]

Mary Keller states that if we, as western academics, continue to correlate the word 'religion' with the word 'belief', we continue to limit our understanding of "religiousness in the modern world". She writes: "those whose religiousness is expressed in their work, in their wars… or in public displays have slid into the anachronistic space of backwardness. They are suspected of being mentally needy because they cannot contain their bubble of belief properly".[7] Kay's diagnosis that her father is indeed insane makes us laugh; it makes us laugh because we are uncomfortable with this inappropriate display of 'religiousness', and made reassuringly comfortable again with Kay's playful diagnosis of her birth father being mentally needy, so we can section this display off into a safe category, mentally ill. But there is a more personal story, with sadness and humour, which goes beyond academic categorisations and theories.

Kay's upbringing as a black child, with white parents, in a predominantly white suburb of Glasgow, gave her an identity of difference, of both wanting to belong and wanting to understand her difference more fully. She describes the moment she arrives in the Igbo village of her ancestors and father. She takes off her shoes and walks down the red dust road:

---

[5] Kay. *Red Dust Road*, 6.
[6] Graham Huggan. *The Postcolonial Exotic: Marketing the Margins* (London: Routledge, 2001), 37.
[7] Mary Keller. *The Hammer and the Flute: Women, Power and Spirit Possession* (Baltimore, MD: John Hopkins University Press, 2002), 7.

> The earth is so copper warm and beautiful and the green of the elephant grasses so lushly green they make me want to weep. I feel such a strong sense of affinity with the colours and the landscape, a strong sense of recognition. There's a feeling of liberation, and exhilaration, that at last, at last, at last I'm here. It feels a million miles from Glasgow, from my lovely Fintry Hills, but, surprisingly, it also feels like home.[8]

But then only hours later, her affinity with the land is shaken as the local villagers, look at her and gather around her saying "Oyibo", meaning white person:

> I spent some of my childhood wishing I was white like the other kids and feeling like I stuck out like a sore thumb; and now in Nigeria, I'm wishing I was black and feeling like I stick out like a sore thumb. It's the first time in my life that I have properly understood what it means being mixed race.[9]

This neither-nor identity, or what W. E. B. DuBois called "double consciousness",[10] leaves Kay searching for her multiple homelands. She is one of many 'hyphenated bodies', to take Vijay Mishra's term,[11] from diasporas across the world. In Kay's case, this trauma is even more astute for it is the personal separation from her birth parents. Jackie Kay's memoir demonstrates and celebrates the complexity of Scottish identity and culture; a place that is aware of its borders, of its imaginary and real homelands scattered around the world, and its relationship with the imperial centre. Jackie Kay allows us to see that its beauty is in its fluid borders and global presence.

---

[8] Kay. *Red Dust Road*, 213.
[9] Ibid. 216.
[10] W.E.B. DuBois. *The Souls of Black Folk* (New York: Dover Publications, [1903] 1994), 2.
[11] Vijay Mishra. "The diasporic imaginary: theorizing the Indian diaspora," *Textual Practice* 10, no.3 (1996): 421 – 447.

Works Cited

DuBois, W.E.B. *The Souls of Black Folk.* New York: Dover Publications, 1903/1994.

Huggan, Graham. *The Postcolonial Exotic: Marketing the Margins.* London: Routledge, 2001.

Kay, Jackie. *Red Dust Road.* London: Picador, 2010.

Kay, Jackie. *The Adoption Papers.* Northumberland: Bloodaxe Books, 1991.

Kay, Jackie. *The Trumpet.* Picador: London, 1998.

Keller, Mary. *The Hammer and the Flute: Women, Power and Spirit Possession*, Baltimore: John Hopkins University Press, 2002.

Mishra, Vijay. "The diasporic imaginary: theorizing the Indian diaspora." *Textual Practice* 10, no. 3 (1996): 421 – 447.

A PROFESSION OF IMAGING RELIGION

Paige M. Medlock

Robert Sowers (1923-1990) created some of the most remarkable stained glass windows in the US during the twentieth century, including the 30,000-panel American Airlines wall at what is now called JFK Airport (formerly Idlewild). His work in 1960 was the largest stained glass window in the world at that time. Terminal 8 stood for forty-eight years then was demolished for remodeling in 2007, and along with it, the enormous window. The New York Times reported that people used to refer to the airport terminal as 'The Cathedral'[1]; ironically, Sowers was a pioneer stained glass artist creating major commissions *outside* the church. It was demolished less than five decades after its commissioning, with suggestions to turn pieces of its glass into key chains for airline employees.

This is quite a contrast from when stained glass reached its height of glory in the medieval period, when the average person would not have much exposure to vibrant colors and use of light outside the church. Their experience *in* the church would have made a physical and spiritual impact.

The actual light translated in illuminated visual images was analogous to the scriptural light of God overcoming the evil or chaos of darkness.

To situate their experience historically, and describe it firsthand: the transition from Romanesque to Gothic architecture, most evidenced in the

---

[1] Ruth Ford. "Demolishing a Celebrated Wall of Glass," last modified 23 July, 2006, https://www.nytimes.com/2006/07/23/nyregion/thecity/23glas.html?_r=1&.

Abbey of St. Denis from the late 12th century under Abbot Suger, who wrote on the theological significance of architectural decisions:

> Thus, when – out of the delight in the beauty of the house of God – the loveliness of the many-coloured gems has called me away from external cares, and worthy meditation has induced me to reflect, transferring that which is material to that which is immaterial, on the diversity of the sacred virtues: then it seems to me that I see myself dwelling, as it were, in some strange region of the universe which neither exists entirely in the slime of the earth nor entirely in the purity of Heaven; and that, by the grace of God, I can be transported from this inferior to that higher world in an anagogical manner.[2]

- Sainte-Chapelle, Paris (photo: P M Medlock)

Later, Gothic architecture achieved verticality and light by developing certain structural elements (pointed arch, rib vaulting, flying buttresses), and this skeletal structure vastly opened up wall space for windows. Stained glass windows were designed to vertical extremes that translated light in color, altering worship atmosphere and illustrating biblical theology. The makers of stained glass knew the limits and possibilities of the material with which they worked in such a way that they could facilitate the optimal brilliance of the finished piece by means of the media. These craftsmen knew not only color theory, but that of glass that permits, prohibits, translates, and radiates light. What would a red piece do next to blue rather than clear when sunlight burns through it? What piece would dominate, or recede, or pierce the air? What combination would

---

[2] Abbot Suger. From "On the Abbey Church of St Denis and Its Art Treasures," in *Theological Aesthetics: A Reader*, ed. Gesa Elsbeth Thiessen (Grand Rapids: William B. Eerdmans Publishing Company, 2005), 116.

confuse or enhance the image and the visual experience? Or the worship experience? What would affect the communication and reception of the image, which was generally a biblical message for the common person unable to read the Word? Gothic stained glass illustrated either the entire bible, as Sainte-Chapelle (pictured) has for eight centuries, or the theme of sinful humanity with hope of salvation through Christ. Alternately, some windows center Christ within purposefully arranged references to other parts of scripture, demonstrating rich theological cross-referencing and skilled thoughtful design.

Two factors led to a major shift in the stained glass profession from its height of glory in the Middle Ages to becoming a 'lost art' in the Renaissance and Reformation. First, art-making became less material-inspired and more imitative of easel painting. Second, iconoclasm ('image breaking') of the Protestant Reformation and Dissolution of Monasteries questioned visual imagery as a scriptural violation rather than theological hermeneutic, and effectively removed stained glass from Christian architecture. But it did not disappear forever.

Sir Herbert Read writes, 'In our own time, as part of a general return to aesthetic integrity, the art of stained glass has been reconsidered and, indeed, rediscovered. The guiding principle of translucency has been re-established, and, as in the Middle Ages, the greatest artists of our time have experimented in this medium.'[3] He could rightly foresee glass as an important element of architecture, an art in itself: hiding unsightly views and coloring space, honoring the integrity of art forms, and turning public spaces into inspiring places. In addition to modern artists such as Matisse and Chagall turning from paint to glass, stained glass of the Craft Movement (especially Morris in England, Mackintosh in Scotland, and Wright in America) restored stained glass from its medieval glory to a contemporary aesthetic, and positioned it as a major element of modern architecture.

Robert Sowers writes, 'When art is working it heightens both the materiality and the fantasy of the image; the two are fused in exaltation. But when the material is excited to no purpose, or the image rooted in no material there can be no deep-rooted art.'[4] His own record-breaking Terminal 8 stained glass window was contracted to Olde Good Glass in New York City to be dismantled and reclaimed into new objects for public

---

[3] Robert Sowers. *The Lost Art: A Survey of One Thousand Years of Stained Glass* (New York: George Wittenborn Inc., 1954), 8.
[4] Sowers. *The Lost Art*, 28.

sale. Was he wrong about the significance of this material and meaning? Stained glass has been installed and removed from religious and secular institutions for seemingly different reasons: sacrilege and outdatedness; it means too much and it means not enough.

Perhaps there is an underlying threat worth questioning that only the material can shed light on: glass is an antithetical, reflective, mediatory material. Isobel Armstrong says we need to work through the paradoxes and contradictions inherent in glass, saying, 'They are perceived at a purely formal or aesthetic level unless they generate a "restlessness", which both reorders a problem and the mind that works on it. This mediation is, in Heidegger's words, "the form of the very thinking which thinks itself". It is "the conceiving of oneself—as the grasping of the not-I"'.[5]

The stained glass process (photo: P M Medlock)

Humans do not like to grasp the not-I, and if stained glass positions the viewer in such tension, even when crafted in awe-inspiring otherworldly visual ways, it may continue to be removed while also being commissioned and installed elsewhere. The stained glass profession has thrived and dwindled, but what it professes will not be extinguished.

The artistic profession of stained glass-making not only revived, but returned its focus to the inherent qualities of the glass. Where stained glass orders chaos by assembling broken pieces into a structured design that illuminates a space with intentionality, it continues to embody the relevance of a timeless yet cutting-edge visual hermeneutic.

---

[5] Isobel Armstrong. *Victorian Glassworlds: Glass Culture and the Imagination 1830-1880* (Oxford: Oxford University Press, 2008), 12.

Works Cited

Ford, Ruth. "Demolishing a Celebrated Wall of Glass." Last modified 23 July, 2006. https://www.nytimes.com/2006/07/23/nyregion/thecity/23glas.html?_r=1&.

Sowers, Robert. *The Lost Art: A Survey of One Thousand Years of Stained Glass*. New York: George Wittenborn Inc., 1954.

Suger, Abbot. From "On the Abbey Church of St Denis and Its Art Treasures." In *Theological Aesthetics: A Reader*, edited by Gesa Elsbeth Thiessen, 114–117. Grand Rapids: William B. Eerdmans Publishing Company, 2005.

BLURRING THE BOUNDARIES – PUNK ROCK AND RELIGION

Francis Stewart

Ever walked into a music shop? What did you find? Most likely you found shelves or boxes—depending on your predilection for large stores or small independents—labelled with types of music found within: metal, jazz, country, rock, pop, opera, classical and everything in between.

Music is often sorted this way on the simple premise that it makes it easier to find the music you want and so increases the likelihood that you will spend money in the store. The danger of presenting music in this manner is that it makes discovery much harder and exploration much less likely. You go straight to the genre you like, find what you want, have a quick look around for anything else in that genre and then head straight to the tills, potentially missing out on undiscovered gems, such as classics that influenced the music you like.

The music genre of punk is replete with subcategories, despite its proponents' love and promotion of various notions of anarchy. Terms such as crusty punk, surfer punk, skater punk, street punk, hardcore punk, 77 punk, and straight edge punk abound. I imagine this is to delineate borders, to define identities, and to attempt to create order and control in a world which can all too easily be wrested from young punks by profit-focused companies. The danger of presenting identity in this manner is that it assumes that identity, behaviour and presentation is rigid and definable. It assumes a shared understanding and therefore tradition of these identity labels and creates a necessary 'other' within a subculture. Finally, it actually results in co-option and control being easier to obtain for large companies.

Identities are fluid and not static as cultural theorists John Storey and Dan Laughey, and sociologist of religion Gordon Lynch have argued. The boundaries between cultural and/or subcultural affiliation have become significantly less rigid and defined. It is now quite common, almost expected, that individuals will merge one or more sometimes disparate identities within their overall sense of self. The multi-faceted sense of self and identity formation is partly a feature of the consumerist, choice-based West, partly a feature of the rise in significance of the self/individual, and partly a result of globalization. This has forced a reconsideration of what we mean, understand and intend in using terms such as 'world religions', 'religion', 'sacred' and 'secular'. From 2009 to 2011, I conducted interviews with straight edge punks in the UK and the USA. 'Straight edge' punks are a subset of punk in which adherents abstain from drugs, alcohol and casual sex. During my interviews, questions of what we mean by terms related to the category of religion were repeatedly raised, discussed in depth and featured prominently in graffiti, tattoos, flyers and band imagery.

As much as punks utilise labels, these labels are carefully chosen and carry a deep significance. Each label denotes an important political or musical derivation that enables deviance and recognition. For example, surfer punk was the term attached to the punks who came from the Huntington Beach area of Orange County USA and were involved with the sport. 'Surfer punk' acknowledged the difficulty and danger of surfing that particular area of the California coast. The ultra-aggressive stance of these punks represented a new culture of physical extremism, which they rode as one would ride a wave. In my research, I wondered if the same careful labelling would be applied to terms and concepts such as 'religion'. During my interviews, a sharp distinction was expressed between 'religion' and 'faith' (UK) or 'spirituality' (USA). This is perhaps unsurprising given the punks stance of rejection of tradition – both real and imagined – in favour of creating something new.

The term 'Religion' was used when interviewees were referring to traditional religious institutions, texts, authority figures and evangelising individuals. In contrast the terms 'faith' and 'spirituality' were used to describe the individual believer(s), specific practices which were not attributable to one religion or another, personal beliefs, and, interestingly, to punk rock itself!

Punk clubs were spoken of as 'sacred spaces' and attendees got agitated with those whose behaviour 'desecrated' this status, in their opinion, or disrespected it. Bands, specific musicians and other individuals important to the local scenes were spoken of with reverence and defended vehemently. Punk rock itself was interpreted as a form of desacralised salvation for many interviewees, and described as a secular yet sacred good with both personal and collective benefits and ramifications. One could argue that the straight edge punk is the result of refusing to accept the boundary between sacred and profane, religious and secular. The movement relies on muddying the waters and blurring the boundaries.

Straight edge punks share many practices—or abstentions—with what one might call 'practicing Christians', like renouncing casual sex, for example, but the Christian community does not appeal to the punks I interviewed who defined religion as practices, rituals, authority figures and to an extent ideology. Charles Taylor writes that neoliberal post-Christian societies are moving from a position of belief in a specific god as the only option available to a belief in any god (or none at all) as one option among many. Concurrently society is wresting authority from the hands of the institutions that function under the auspices of the divine, placing it instead in secular institutions and communities. We now face a vast range of human practices which are overlapping and do not function as religious or secular solely or discreetly.

Much like a growing subculture or indeed a music shop, we have to ask, are new labels now needed, or can we do away with labels once and for all? The punk ethos of "question everything, accept nothing" seems somewhat apt here!

Works Cited

Laughey, Dan. *Music and Youth Culture*. Edinburgh: Edinburgh University Press, 2006.

Lynch, Gordon. *After Religion: 'Generation X' and the Search for Meaning*. London: Darton-Longman-Todd, 2002.

Storey, John. *An Introduction to Cultural Theory and Popular Culture*. Essex: Prentice Hall / Harvester Wheatsheaf, 1997.

Taylor, Charles. *A Secular Age*. Harvard: Belknap Press, 2007.

LOGIC, POETRY, AND THE MYTH OF DISENCHANTMENT

Melanie Barbato

In this short article I will discuss some issues surrounding the use of formalized repetitions and the "disenchantment" of language in modern times.

Robert Yelle has shown in his book *The Language of Disenchantment* (2013) that the attempts of the British civilizing mission to roll back mantras and other apparently non-rational forms of language in India had a precursor in the polemics against Catholic "vain repetitions" back home:

> Protestant iconoclasm at a deep level informed many criticisms of Hindu culture, beginning with its worship of multiple gods or images (murti) of these in stone metal, or wood. […] These polemics were in many instances simply transferred from Catholics to Hindus as their target, with little if any modification. Such was the case not only with the worship of images, but also with attacks on the various forms of chants that Hindus used – mantras, Vedic recitation (svadhyaya), and the like – which, to many British, resembled the chanting of the Ave Maria by Catholics."[1]

---

[1] Robert Yelle. *The Language of Disenchantment* (Oxford: Oxford University Press, 2013), 9.

According Yelle, "disenchantment" was an ideology, not an historical process that did happen or could have happened. The interesting question is therefore not how language got disenchanted but how disenchantment is employed as a rhetorical tool in narratives of approaching the other. An example from Indian logic can show how fluid the boundaries between aesthetics, religious belief and rational argumentation can be. When Western scholars learned about the traditional five step inference model of the Indian Nyaya school, they considered it as inferior to the three step Aristotelian model because of the apparently redundant repetitions of the form. H.N. Randle in his "A Note on the Indian Syllogism" called the Indian model "an untidy organism [...] with vestigial structures and rudimentary organs", especially when compared to the "more perfect work of art, the Aristotelian syllogism".[2] It is true that the Nyaya inference model requires apparently superfluous examples and repetitive steps:

Proposition: This mountain is fire-possessing.
Reason: Because it is smoke-possessing.
Example: Like the kitchen, unlike the lake.
Application: This mountain, since it possesses smoke, possesses fire.
Conclusion: This mountain is fire-possessing.

Both the examples and the repetitions can be explained if the background of Indian logic is taken into account. Logic in India was fundamentally rooted in rhetoric, and the goal was to guide the audience or the other party of the debate along every step of the argument so that they could follow and, if in an amicable mood, agree with every single point. Repetitions were not seen as a flaw. On the contrary, Jainas considered the elaborate ten-step syllogism as found in the writings of Bhadrabahu the highest form of making an argument, superior to the five step model. A three step argument was also known to Nyaya logic, but was considered only suitable for drawing conclusions for oneself, not for convincing others.[3]

While oral culture relies on formalized repetitions for both effect and style, for the British, logic had to conform to their preference for plain style and classicist aesthetics. For Randle, the Aristotelean syllogism was after all

---

[2] H.N. Randle. "A Note on the Indian Syllogism" (Abingdon: Routledge, 1924/2001), 75.
[3] For more on this see the chapter on Indian Logic in Melanie Barbato, *Jain Approaches to Plurality* (2017).

not only "perfect" but also a "work of art". Poetry, maybe the most obvious "word-art", is today also dominated by the preference for non-repetitive forms. The argument is that poetry has been freed from the straight jacket of rhyme, form and metre.[4] Rhyme, the regular correspondence of sounds, seems to be for modern ears a particularly vain, if not ridiculous, repetition. The first rule of Frank L. Visco's famous (and now viral) list of "How to Write Good" reads "Avoid Alliteration. Always". Like the difference between Protestant plain style and the repetitiveness of Indian mantras or the Catholic rosary, this is not just an aesthetic preference. By using rhyme, poetry can recreate, reaffirm and conform to a given order. The fact that form and rhyme are out of favour on the poetry market can therefore be taken to reflect a more general individualization and the rejection of traditional pattern in many areas of life.

It is not a coincidence then that the revival of poetical formalism was called for in particular by Catholics. In 1987 the Catholic poet and critic Dana Gioia criticized modern mainstream poetry for the "debasement of poetic language; [...] the inability to establish a meaningful aesthetic for new poetic narrative and the denial of a musical texture in the contemporary poem."[5] He called for a renewed interest in the aural aspects of poetry that had been replaced by the more visual and text-centred focus of contemporary free verse. Metre, which Gioia (1987: 396) understood as dating back to times "when there was little, if any, distinction between poetry, religion, history, music and magic",[6] was taken by new formalism as part of the solution. Unsurprisingly, new formalism has been called "patriarchal" and a "dangerous nostalgia". But while alliteration may not always be awesome, free verse is just as dangerous in the sense of promoting a particular blend of "political" or "religious" preferences. In either direction, shifts in how language is supposed to be used can tell a lot about power relations but they do not in themselves constitute a form of "progress".

Like other judgements that are called aesthetic, political, religious or rational, they are mingled with the myths we have come to hold true.

---

[4] See the discussion in Suzanne W. Churchill. *The Little Magazine Others and the Renovation of Modern American Poetry* (2006).

[5] Dana Goia. "Notes on the New Formalism", *The Hudson Review: A Magazine of Literature and the Arts*, XL, no. 3 (Autumn 1987), 408.

[6] Goia. "Notes on the New Formalism", 396.

Works Cited

Barbato, Melanie, *Jain Approaches to Plurality: Identity as Dialogue*. Leiden: Brill, 2017.

Churchill, Suzanne W., *The Little Magazine Others and the Renovation of Modern American Poetry*, Aldershot: Routledge, 2006.

Goia, Dana, "Notes on the New Formalism." *The Hudson Review: A Magazine of Literature and the Arts* XL, no. 3 (Autumn 1987): 395-408.

Randle, H.N., "A Note on the Indian Syllogism", 1924, republished in Jonardon Ganeri, *Indian Logic: A Reader*. Abingdon: Routledge, 2001, 75-92.

Yelle, Robert, *The Language of Disenchantment: Protestant Literalism and Colonial Discourse in British India*. Oxford: Oxford University Press, 2012.

CRITICAL RELIGION AND POLITICS

"THE DISCOURSE ON GOOD AND BAD SECULARISM: A CONTEMPORARY GENEALOGY OF SECULARISM IN FRANCE."

Per-Erik Nilsson

The year was 1989 when a scandal occurred that quickly turned into a national affair.[1] Three teenaged Muslim girls were expelled from their public high school in a city north of Paris for wearing veils on the school's premises. During the following months national and local press, radio, and television reported this event as if nothing else mattered in France. These girls' veils were articulated as the emblem of an imagined patriarchal Islamic Orient taking root in the midst of France.[2] In the conservative daily, one of the many headlines read: "The War of the Veil."[3]

One side of this war was represented by the Islamic veil, the other by secularism (*laïcité*). Slowly a new republican consensus was formed.

---

[1] See John Bowen. *Why the French Don't Like Headscarves: Islam, the State, and Public Space* (Princeton and Oxford: Princeton University Press, 2007); Joan W. Scott. *Politics of the Veil* (Oxford and Princeton: Princeton University Press, 2007).

[2] See Joan Scott. *Sex and Secularism* (Oxford and Princeton: Princeton University Press, 2018).

[3] Per-Erik Nilsson. *Unveiling the French Republic* (Leiden: Brill, 2017), 48.

Secularism, which earlier had divided the republican left from the conservative and, most often, the Catholic right[4] came to be regarded as the essential emblem of France, as a teleological spirit that had been guiding the Republic to liberty, equality, and fraternity. Secularism was simultaneously, and often contradictorily, articulated as a value base founded by a principle of integration, a legal foundation, based on the separation of Church and State in 1905, and the guarantee of separating "religion" from politics. Some rooted the genesis of secularism in Enlightenment thought, some in the Gospel of Matthew, 22:21 ("Render to Caesar the things that are Caesar's; and to God the things that are God's").

Whatever secularism was taken to mean, the Islamic veil was not compatible with it. In 2004 the National Assembly legislated against conspicuous religious symbols in public schools and, in 2010, against full-face coverage in public space. Early on it became clear that these two laws were targeting the hijab, in 2004, and the niqab, in 2010. However, the communist MP André Gerin, who was a leading figure in the legislation of 2010, stated that the niqab was only the tip of the iceberg of a much larger problem.[5] A broad range of society's ills were attributed to "bad" Islam; i.e. Muslims who were transgressing its proscribed private place. One may ask in exactly what ways Muslims were doing this, besides being visible in public space either by wearing Islamic garments, or by simply "looking" like a Muslim. Secularism, here, started to emerge as a shibboleth of being French; as the former president Nicolas Sarkozy stated: "Those who do not respect the French way of secularism are not welcome on the territory of the French Republic. This is France."[6]

With the many Jihadi attacks in France, most notably with the attack against the satirical newspaper *Charlie Hebdo* and the Jewish supermarket Hyper Casher as well as the devastating attack against the concert hall Bataclan and surrounding restaurants and bars in 2015, secularism once again came to the fore.[7] It now started being incorporated into the

---

[4] See Jean Baubérot. *Laïcité 1905–2005, entre passion et raison* (Paris: Editions Seuil, 2004).

[5] Nilsson, *Unveiling*, 146.

[6] Nicolas Sarkozy. *Discours du Président de la République. Epinal*, 12 July 2007, *Palais de l'Élysée*, Paris. Secularism was moreover turned into a prerequisite in the French integration contract applying to third-country nationals as stipulated in the *Code de l'entrée et de séjour des étrangers et du droit d'asile*. Nilsson, Unveiling, 188-189.

[7] See Per-Erik Nilsson. "Where's Charlie? The Discourse on Religious Violence and Discursive Displacement in France Post-7/1 2015, in *The Cambridge Companion to Religion and Terrorism*, edited by James R. Lewis (Cambridge: Cambridge University Press, 2017).

Republic's anti-terrorism strategies. In 2018, PM Édouard Phillippe presented the government's new anti-radicalization plan "*Prévenir pour protéger: Plan national de prevention de la radicalization.*" In the plan, secularism is presented as a cure for radicalisation as well as a shield against unwanted alterity. Parallel to these developments, secularism has started to be appropriated by those that, up until recently, had been adversaries of secularism. In 2006 and later in 2011 Marine Le Pen, the new leader of the *Rassemblement National* (formerly *Front National*), declared that she was the real defender of secularism. In the same time period French Identitarians and other radical nationalists came out as the true secularists, coated in Christian symbolism, and equated secularism to a *reconquista*, a strategy to purify the nation from the supposed ills of Islam and Muslims.[8]

Meanwhile, public intellectuals and scholars have been seeking to tackle the multifaceted aspects of secularism: What is it really? During the last decade, a vast array of historical analysis, popular literature, cartoons, as well as manuals, and guides have been sent from publishers to book stores around the country, all seeking to explain how to understand and live according to the standards of secularism in daily and professional life. For example, the philosopher Henri-Pena Ruiz in his *Le dictionnaire amoureux de la Laïcité* holds that "loving secularism is loving an ideal that applies to all."[9] Secularism appears as an ideal meriting love, but also as an ideal that can be betrayed.

In a recent book the eminent scholar of French secularism (*laïcité*), Jean Baubérot, expresses concern for what he considers to be a falsified "secularism."[10] Baubérot's concern is similar to that of Western political leaders and intellectuals who portray Islam as a "religion" that can be hijacked and used by fundamentalists for political and mischievous purposes.[11] However, to Baubérot it is not Islamic fundamentalists that are the perpetrators. Instead, as Baubérot suggests, the perpetrators are the aforementioned French conservatives and radical nationalists. As Baubérot would have it, secularism has been *UMPLepinized* (a neologism of the then

---

[8] See Per-Erik Nilsson. *French Populism and Discourses on Secularism* (London and New York: Bloomsbury, 2018).

[9] Henri-Pena Ruiz. *Le dictionnaire amoreux de la laïcité* (Paris: Plon, 2014), 16.

[10] Jean Baubérot. *La laïcité falsifiée* (Paris: La Découverte, 2012).

[11] See Arun Kundnani. "Islamism and the Roots of Liberal Rage," *Race & Class*, 50(2) 2008: 40-68; Raphaël Liogier. *Le Mythe de l'islamisation, essai sur une obsession collective* (Paris: Seuil, 2012); Mahmood Mamdani. *Good Muslim, Bad Muslim. America and the Cold War, and the Roots of Terror* (New York: Pantheon Books, 2004).

conservative party *Union pour un mouvement populaire,* today *Les Républicains*, and Le Pen). Baubérot informs us how these parties have managed to twist secularism into something hostile towards Islam and Muslims, which is supposedly contrary to its original meaning.

This falsification has occurred during the aforementioned "Islamic Affairs" that have been occupying the media and the political center in France for the last 25 years or so. Indeed, the conservatives and radical nationalists have appropriated secularism in a seemingly new manner. However, I find it curious that this supposed falsification is portrayed as a rupture in an otherwise liberating, historical unfolding of secularism.

To explain the logic in play let us consider a similar case. In the 2014 European Parliament Election special by the leftist daily *La Libération,* the journalists Jonathan Bouchet-Petersen and Antoine Guiral analysed the success of Marine Le Pen and stated: "To France, country of human rights, the symbol of FN in the lead is a blot."[12] As if France, the country of the colonial civilizing mission par excellence, the Dreyfus Affair, the Vichy Régime, the drowning of Algerian protesters in Paris by the police in 1962, the recent anti-terrorist laws and policies targeting Muslim citizens, the extra-legal detention centers for third country nationals, the violent Roma expulsions, and so on, has only *now* betrayed the imagined and glorified heritage of human rights.

Now, to put secularism back on track, to stop its falsification, Baubérot urges us to go back to its roots and fully apply the famous Law of 1905 separating Church and State; or, as I understand it from Baubérot's writings, the foundational Law of Secularism.[13] However, as Baubérot himself has pointed out, as have many other scholars, the Law of 1905 separating the Church from the State was unequally applied in the French colonial empire. In French Algeria, its non-application to the Muslim population led to a tutelage role of the state in relation to Muslims and practised Islam, meaning that the state could keep Algerian mosques on a tight leash. Muslims, moreover, were not given the status of full citizens and were deemed incapable of being secular. Not only did this contribute to making "Muslim"

---

[12] Antine Guiral and Jonathan Bouchet-Petersen. "Des élections entre Europé et haine," *Libération,* 24 May 2014, accessed 15 January 2019, https://www.liberation.fr/france/2014/05/25/des-elections-entre-europe-et-haine_1026814.

[13] See Amélie Barras. "Secularism in France", in *The Oxford handbook of Secularism,* edited by Phil Zuckerman and John R. Shook (Oxford: Oxford University Press, 2017): 142–154.

an ethnic marker, it also rendered "secular" as a marker for Christian Europeans.[14]

Thus, if secularism has a proper history as a particular phenomenon (as I understand Baubérot's writings), I wonder what the differences are between contemporary and historical secularism? For sure, in metropolitan France the Law of 1905 targeted the Catholic Church's influence on the French Republic; however, Muslim Algeria was also a part of France. This makes me wonder if a historical continuity can be ascribed to secularism. Does not secularism from its very birth become a marker of identity for the secular, the non-secular, and the potentially secular as well as a political technique to police and govern the borders in between?

The desire to find an untainted historical secularism leads to an idealized and normative analysis rendering power and ideology secondary. Instead of properly understanding how the category of secularism functions and in what kind of power relations the category is given a role, one easily slips into an anachronistic discussion on the shoulds-and-should-nots of secularism; i.e. into a discourse on good and bad secularism all too reminiscent of the discourse on good and bad religion. When secularism becomes an a-historical and an a-political truth, and turns into a battle of who is the most secular, or the mostly correct secular, it casts a shadow over the exercise of violence legitimated in its name.

---

[14] See Franck Frégosi. *Penser l'islam dans la laïcité* (Paris: Fayard, 2008).

Works Cited

Barras, Amélie. "Secularism in France." In *The Oxford handbook of Secularism*, edited by Phil Zuckerman and John R. Shook, 142–154. Oxford: Oxford University Press, 2017.

Baubérot, Jean. *Laïcité 1905–2005, entre passion et raison*. Paris: Editions Seuil, 2004.

Bowen, John. *Why the French Don't Like Headscarves: Islam, the State, and Public Space*. Princeton and Oxford: Princeton University Press, 2007.

Frégosi, Franck. *Penser l'islam dans la laïcité*. Paris: Fayard, 2008.

Guiral, Antine and Jonathan Bouchet-Petersen. "Des élections entre Europé et haine." *Libération*, 24 May 2014. Accessed 15 January 2019. https://www.liberation.fr/france/2014/05/25/des-elections-entre-europe-et-haine_1026814

Kundnani, Arun. "Islamism and the Roots of Liberal Rage." *Race & Class* 50, no.2 (2008): 40-68.

Liogier, Raphaël. *Le Mythe de l'islamisation, essai sur une obsession collective*. Paris: Seuil, 2012.

Mamdani, Mahmood. Good Muslim, Bad Muslim. America and the Cold War, and the Roots of Terror. New York: Pantheon Books, 2004.

Nilsson, Per-Erik. "Where's Charlie? The Discourse on Religious Violence and Discursive Displacement in France Post-7/1 2015. In The Cambridge Companion to Religion and Terrorism, edited by James R. Lewis, 191-202. Cambridge: Cambridge University Press, 2017.

Nilsson, Per-Erik. French Populism and Discourses on Secularism (London and New York: Bloomsbury, 2018).

Nilsson, Per-Erik. Unveiling the French Republic. Leiden: Brill, 2017.

Ruiz, Henri-Pena. *Le dictionnaire amoreux de la laïcité*. Paris: Plon, 2014.

Nicolas Sarkozy. *Discours du Président de la République: Epinal*. 12 July 2007, *Palais de l'Élysée*, Paris. Accessed 10 June 2020: https://www.vie-publique.fr/discours/167260-declaration-de-m-nicolas-sarkozy-president-de-la-republique-sur-le-ro.

Scott, Joan W. *Politics of the Veil*. Oxford and Princeton: Princeton University Press, 2007.

Scott, Joan. *Sex and Secularism*. Oxford and Princeton: Princeton University Press, 2018.

'RELIGION' AND THE STUDY OF 'RELIGIOUS LEADERSHIP': SOME OBSERVATIONS FROM LEBANON

Alexander Henley

The distinctive thing about religious leadership is that it is religious. The clue is in the name. Nor do religious leaders themselves let us forget it, setting themselves apart from non-religious leaders and the general public by means of their outlandish dress, their publicly pious practices, their religious expressions and references, and even their personal grooming habits. The very obviousness of this religious nature leads to assumptions of a difference between religious and non-religious leaders that goes far deeper than appearances. In the case of Lebanon, where religious leaders of various Muslim and Christian stripes wield a great deal of power, such assumptions have become so essential to the expression of secular modernist ideals that I devoted my doctoral research to exploring them. Here I will outline a few of the misconceptions I have encountered, some or all of which may be familiar in other contexts.

Religious leadership is one of several categories of actor treated regularly in general works on politics in Lebanon. For example, a recent book by Rola el-Husseini includes this conventional section in a chapter on non-state elites more broadly: 'Whereas state elites act directly within the political arena…

these unelected elites' influence the political arena from 'the shadows'.[1] 'The Role of the Clergy in Politics' begins by setting the scene:

> The clergy has always had an impact on political life in Lebanon owing to the confessional nature of the country's political allegiances. Indeed, the concept of national citizenship has not taken hold in Lebanon in the same way that it has in Western nations. Loyalty to the family, the clan, and the religious community overrides other allegiances, leaving little room for national patriotism.[2]

Here the category of religion – including religious actors ('the clergy') and 'religious community' – is taken to be self-explanatory, a natural and permanent feature of the social universe. Further, religious phenomena are contrasted with modern structures and concepts of nation, state and citizenship, as both their precursors and their presumed opponents.

Framing 'religious leadership' as a generic category within a religious-secular binary seems common sense, and prompts certain kinds of common sense questions: Why has the rise of secular political leadership in a modernising state like Lebanon not resulted in the decline of religious leadership, as the secularisation thesis would have us expect? Conversely, under what conditions do religious leaders become politicised? Attempts to answer such questions, well-intentioned as they may be, serve to obscure or mystify all sorts of power dynamics at work within and across the binary they take for granted.

Religion-and-Politics studies like these tend to obscure difference among 'religious leaders' (merging diverse histories and functions into 'The Role of the Clergy') as well as obscuring similarity between 'religious' and 'political' actors (both of which may be elected, depend on state recognition, and promote national patriotism – all characteristics el-Husseini uses to distinguish 'state elites' from 'non-state elites' such as 'the clergy').

In the process, they tend to obscure historical change (flattening the divergent pasts and disguising the often-recent origins of 'traditional clerics committed to a time-honored religious hierarchy')[3] as well as mystifying present motivations (which may be explained in terms of reified religious

---
[1] Rola el-Husseini. *Pax Syriana: Elite Politics in Postwar Lebanon* (Syracuse, NY: Syracuse University Press, 2012), 122.
[2] el-Husseini. *Pax Syriana*, 140.
[3] Ibid. 141.

'tradition' extracted from pre-modern history). Classifying actors as essentially either 'religious' or 'political' leads scholars to judge them according to imposed criteria of sincerity that mystify the actors' own intentions and obscure the power of their own discursive framing: what does it really mean to say that a 'religious leader' may 'become politicized' whereas a 'leader who is first and foremost a politician' may 'borrow the symbolism of religion'?[4]

Several general theories have been proposed to answer questions about the 'persistence' of powerful religious leadership in countries like Lebanon. Fiona McCallum summarizes three common theories as follows.[5] One view is that Oriental religions – both Islam and by extension Eastern branches of Christianity – are by nature more resistant to secularization than European Christianity. Another links the failure of secularisation to the weakness of the state: if people do not find security in the modern state, they look to their traditional leaders instead. A third refers to a religious resurgence that is part of a reaction against globalization. Sometimes one or other of these theories appears to fit a particular religious institution or community at a particular time, but they all fail to give the kind of generalizable explanation that they claim to provide. The problem is in the way research projects are formulated around the category 'religion'.

In formulating my own comparative study of religious leaders in modern Lebanon, I was once warned that the task was not only inadvisable but likely impossible: each religious community is 'like a different country' and must be understood through its own history and religious tradition. Other well-meaning advisers suggested that to study religious leaders was in fact to study vestiges of a pre-modern past, not the 'modern politics' that are the stuff of Lebanon's present and future. The category of religion has in practice led researchers to focus on individual religious communities as independent spheres of action that can (and should) be understood separately from each other and from the modern context of the state – while concomitantly making assumptions about the universality of religious phenomena.

As well as using cases of religious leadership to draw generalised conclusions about religion, the tendency to circumscribe scholarship on each religion has also produced an alternative approach that uses the

---

[4] Ibid. 140, 141.
[5] Fiona McCallum. *Christian Religious Leadership in the Middle East* (Lampeter: Edwin Mellen Press, 2010). Chapter 1.

particularities of different religions or sects to explain the roles of their religious leaders.[6] For example, Sunni Islam is said to be characterised by the overlap of religion and state, so the Lebanese Sunni Mufti, who is salaried from the state budget, is considered a relic of the privileged place of Sunnis in Islamic Empires. Lebanese Shi'ite leadership, by contrast, was only set up in the late 1960s by populist Imam Musa al-Sadr, and tends to be linked to a regional 'Shi'ite awakening' of a latent revolutionary tendency in Shi'ism. And Druze sheikhs have always had a central role, it is said, because of the insular, tribal character of Druze religion, which has clung to its traditions despite centuries of persecution. Such explanations often lead, in my view, to an uncritical reproduction of clichés, which risks feeding prejudices.

These conventional narratives – whether of religious particularism or of religion in general – project essentialised images of religion(s) onto actual social formations, and in doing so obscure the modern historical context. So going back to the three examples above, they appear in a very different light when viewed in relation to one another and to the modern state. It was only in the 1930s and 40s that a Mufti was elevated above other clerics in response to the colonial state's demand for religious representatives, becoming a national figurehead for a newly defined Sunni community. The Shi'ite leadership may have been created later, but was designed to match the Sunni model at the height of its national prestige. Meanwhile the Druze community, like the Sunnis, adapted an existing Druze sheikhly title to generate their own equivalent of the Mufti that has gradually displaced competing modes of leadership.

Once viewed comparatively, it becomes clear that these various institutions have been shaped into their modern forms by the context of the Lebanese state and its new multi-confessional public sphere, in which 'religious leadership' has acquired the meaning we now take for granted.[7] Yet explanations of their contemporary prominence continue to hinge on their supposed natural connection with 'primordial' allegiances among the population.

---

[6] A classic example is Fouad Khuri. *Imams and Emirs: State, Religion and Sects in Islam* (London: Saqi Books, 1990).

[7] Alexander Henley. "Remaking the Mosaic: Religious Leaders and Secular Borders in the Colonial Levant", *Religion and Society* 6/1 (2015), 155-168; "Between Sect and State in Lebanon: Religious Leaders at the Interface", *Journal of Islamic and Muslim Studies* 1/1 (2016), 1-11.

An essential distinction is conventionally drawn between the Lebanese communities' 'secular' and 'religious' spokesmen. Ironically, it has not been uncommon for commentators to judge the 'religious' leaders more representative than their 'secular' counterparts. A classic text of the 1960s popularised the idea that religious leaders comprised a 'shadow parliament' able to express raw sectarian viewpoints that were excluded from Parliament by the moderating effect of the electoral process.[8]

Confused perceptions of an organic connection between religious leadership and religious community result in these figures being linked to sectarianism as both a product and a cause. On one hand they are assumed to 'resonate' in some mystical way with their coreligionists;[9] on the other, they are accused of retarding Lebanon's development from sectarianism to nationalism through their undemocratic interference in politics.

My own study finds that the official 'religious leaders' of each sect are sustained above all by the state's recognition and legislation of their roles. Indeed, taking a closer look at the way they actually use this public platform, we see a discourse heavily imbued with the 'national patriotism' el-Husseini despaired of, aimed not at inciting sectarian rivalry but responsible citizenship and submission to a strong central state.[10]

One of the reasons their role is so misunderstood is that commentators dismiss what they have to say because it is delivered in 'religious' terms, couched in the preaching of moral values. Whether the clerics' pacific 'religious' discourse is suspected of insincerity – public platitudes covering for private support of militancy – or considered naïvely well-intentioned, the assumption being made is that such discourse is ineffective, detached from real power politics. Once again the isolation of religion as a category obscures very real power dynamics, especially the negotiation of knowledge across the imaginary religious-secular divide. 'Religious leaders' are no less part of the contemporary systems of meaning that define the salience of leadership, citizenship, and national belonging; their own roles are articulated in these terms, and like others they participate in the interpretation of the language that shapes the Lebanese public sphere.

---

[8] Leila Meo. *Lebanon: Improbable Nation* (Bloomington: Indiana University Press, 1965), 55.

[9] Edmond Rabbat. La formation historique du Liban politique et constitutionnel (Beirut: Université Libanaise, 1986), 93.

[10] Alexander Henley. "Religious Nationalism in the Official Culture of Multi-Confessional Lebanon", in *The Struggle to Define a Nation: Rethinking Religious Nationalism in the Contemporary Islamic World*, eds. M. Demichelis and P. Maggiolini (Piscataway, NJ: Gorgias Press, 2017), 17-44.

Works Cited

el-Husseini, Rola. *Pax Syriana: Elite Politics in Postwar Lebanon*. Syracuse, NY: Syracuse University Press, 2012.

Henley, Alexander. "Remaking the Mosaic: Religious Leaders and Secular Borders in the Colonial Levant". *Religion and Society* 6, no. 1 (2015), 155-168.

Henley, Alexander. "Between Sect and State in Lebanon: Religious Leaders at the Interface". *Journal of Islamic and Muslim Studies* 1, no. 1 (2016), 1-11.

Henley, Alexander. "Religious Nationalism in the Official Culture of Multi-Confessional Lebanon". In *The Struggle to Define a Nation: Rethinking Religious Nationalism in the Contemporary Islamic World*, edited by M. Demichelis and P. Maggiolini, 17-44. (Piscataway, NJ: Gorgias Press, 2017.

Khuri, Fouad. *Imams and Emirs: State, Religion and Sects in Islam*. London: Saqi Books, 1990.

McCallum, Fiona. *Christian Religious Leadership in the Middle East*. Lampeter: Edwin Mellen Press, 2010.

Meo, Leila. *Lebanon: Improbable Nation*. Bloomington: Indiana University Press, 1965.

Rabbat, Edmond. *La formation historique du Liban politique et constitutionnel*. Beirut: Université Libanaise, 1986.

TIBETAN SELF-IMMOLATION BETWEEN RELIGIOUS PRACTICE AND POLITICAL STATEMENT

Carolina Ivanescu

The first self-immolation in Tibetan society in the modern era took place in exile in Delhi, India in 1998 as the Indian police broke up a Tibetan Youth Congress hunger strike. Since then, five more Tibetans have set fire to themselves in exile and a growing number continue to do so in what is considered the occupied territory of Tibet. Since February 2009 more than 100 Tibetans have set themselves of fire within the Tibetan Autonomous Region (TAR).[1] Tibet itself is on fire The Economist calls out,[2] pointing at the magnitude of these individual acts if taken all together. According to such a view self-immolations enact the 'burning issue' of the Tibetan issue in order to remind the world about the situation of Tibetans and their long history of exile. But are self-immolations political acts or are they the expression of religious ideals? While the self-immolations have a clear political goal, dramatically calling for attention towards Tibetans from the western world they are also religious acts, deeply embedded in Tibetan

---

[1] "Self-immolation protests: How does China respond to self-immolation protests?," *freeTibet*, accessed on 4.04.2013, http://www.freetibet.org/news-media/na/full-list-self-immolations-tibet.

[2] "Self-immolation in Tibet: the burning issue," *The Economist*, 9.12.2012, accessed on 10.06.2020, https://www.economist.com/analects/2012/12/09/the-burning-issue.

Buddhism. That seems to be a paradox, because how can a religion that deeply discourages violence agree with such an extreme form of suicide?

It cannot be contested that self-immolations are political in nature. Indeed many initiators of such acts call for unity within Tibet: You must unite and work together to build a strong and prosperous Tibetan nation in the future. This is the sole wish of all the Tibetan heroes.[3] In the view of those who agree with this political statement unity is needed in front of the divisive policies of the Chinese government and also in front of the disagreement of how to approach Tibetan independence from exile. The later extrapolates between the non-violent approach which for the past half of a century has been advocated and implemented under the authority of the Dalai Lama and the more impatient approach of Tibetan youth who feel that non-violence is not an answer.

Violence committed towards the self is not only the middle way between these two options, as it might at first seem. It is a practice that is embedded if not encouraged by Tibetan Buddhism and its ideas of ultimate giving, selflessness, sacrifice of the self for the others. The religious expression of these ideas is the ritual of gCod where the symbolic sacrifice of the body is used as a way of severing attachment to existence.[4] But an even more pronounced expression of the value of self-sacrifice can be found in Shantideva's Bodhisattvacharyavatara, a text often taught at public occasions by the Dalai Lama. This text explains in details the attributes and actions of a bodhisattva, the enlightened being who is working for the benefit of other. Here the exchange of the self for others is a main idea:

> At the beginning, the Guide of the World encourages/ The giving of such things as food' Later, when accustomed to this,/One may progressively start to give away even one's flesh.[5]

In this perception the renunciation to the body and to the flesh symbolizes the renunciation to the self. The self, accompanied by a feeling of individuation is considered the highest impediment on the spiritual path.

---

[3] "Harrowing images and last message from Tibet of first lama to self-immolate," *International Campaign for Tibet*, accessed on 5.04.2013, https://www.savetibet.org/harrowing-images-and-last-message-from-tibet-of-first-lama-to-self-immolate/.

[4] David Stott. "Offering the body: The practice of gCod in Tibetan Buddhism," *Religion* 19, no. 3 (1989): 221-226.

[5] Acharya Shantideva. "Guide to the Bodhisattva's Way of Life," trans. Stephen Batchelor (Dharamsala: Library of Tibetan Works and Archives, 1979), 63.

In order to reach enlightenment the self and its importance must be diminished or destroyed. This can be done through meditative practices but also rather literal forms of self-sacrifice. While in order to attain spiritual benefit renunciation to the self must take place as an offering to the benefit of others, it is foremost the one who makes the sacrifice who reaps the benefits. In this way, as the Dalai Lama turns the argument around, caring for others is the way of being truly selfish. Thus, by sacrificing oneself one can be truly selfish: through thinking only of others and sacrificing the self for others, one can actually reach high spiritual attainment.[6]

However, it is not the promise of spiritual attainment that motivates Tibetan self-immolators. Rather it is the ideal of collective freedom and independence that motivates these acts. Although these two seem like they are articulating a political goal, transforming self-sacrifice into a political act, once more religious and political goals are cross-fertilizing each other. Many Tibetans who have contributed to a burning Tibet express a wish for Tibetan unity, wishing to be free to practice Tibetan Buddhism and listen to the teachings of the Dalai Lama.[7] Meanwhile, however, they become heroes who apply in practice the ideal of the bodhisattva while fighting for their rights towards religious identity and practice. With this attitude self-immolations make a superior moral claim upon collective freedom and independence, making it difficult for the Chinese to respond.

Although self-sacrifice through fire is unique neither to Asian cultures nor to Buddhism, the specific intersection of political and religious goals in the Tibetan context is unique. Tibetan self-immolations are actions taken for the welfare and benefit of others. This presents a special case to Talal Asad's approach in which he considers the religious and political as mutually defining each other.[8] The case of Tibetan self-immolations throws light on the way categories of religion and politics are constructed and implemented as a transnational political statement made with the help of acts of compassion. The heroism of Tibetans rests on the moral superiority of their political statements that are backed up by religious principles of ultimate renunciation.

---

[6] Dalai Lama and Howard C. Cutler. *The art of happiness at work* (London: Hodder & Stoughton, 1999).

[7] "Storm in the Grasslands: Self-immolations in Tibet and Chinese policy," *International Campaign for Tibet*, accessed on 8.04.2013, http://www.savetibet.org/resource-center/ict-publications/reports/storm-grasslands-self-immolations-tibet-and-chinese-policy.

[8] Talal Asad. *Genealogies of religion: Discipline and reasons of power in Christianity and Islam*, (Baltimore, MD: JHU Press, 2003).

Works Cited

Acharya Shantideva. *Guide to the Bodhisattva's Way of Life.* Translated by Stephen Batchelor. Dharamsala: Library of Tibetan Works and Archives 1979.

Asad, Talal. *Genealogies of Religion: Discipline and Reasons of Power in Christianity and Islam.* Baltimore: JHU Press, 2003.

Dalai Lama and Cutler, Howard C. *The Art of Happiness at Work.* London: Hodder & Stoughton, 1999.

freeTibet. " Self-immolation protests: How does China respond to self-immolation protests?." Accessed on 4 April 2013. http://www.freetibet.org/news-media/na/full-list-self-immolations-tibet

International Campaign for Tibet. " Harrowing images and last message from Tibet of first lama to self-immolate." Accessed on 5 April 2013. https://www.savetibet.org/harrowing-images-and-last-message-from-tibet-of-first-lama-to-self-immolate/.

International Campaign for Tibet. " Storm in the Grasslands: Self-immolations in Tibet and Chinese policy." *International Campaign for Tibet.* Accessed on 8 April 2013. http://www.savetibet.org/resource-center/ict-publications/reports/storm-grasslands-self-immolations-tibet-and-chinese-policy.

Stott, David. "Offering the body: The practice of gCod in Tibetan Buddhism." *Religion* 19, no. 3 (1989): 221-226.

The Economist. "Self-immolation in Tibet: the burning issue." 9.12.2012. Accessed on 10.06.2020. https://www.economist.com/analects/2012/12/09/the-burning-issue.

CRITICAL POLITICS

Timothy Fitzgerald

The blog of the Critical Religion Association, for which this piece was originally written, has published contributions from many people, and they usually have the terms 'critical' and 'religion' in them somewhere. Some are much more clearly theorised than that. My own understanding of 'critical religion' is specific. For me, 'critical religion' is always about 'religion and related categories', because I argue that religion is not a stand-alone category, but is one of a configuration of categories. On its own, 'religion' has no object; it only seems to do so. Religion is a category that is deployed for purposes of classification, but it does not stand in a one-to-one relationship with any observable thing in the world. In modern discourse, 'religion' works as half a binary, as in 'religion and secular' or 'religion and [secular] politics'. When we talk about religion today, there is always a tacit *exclusion* of whatever is considered to be non-religious. If, for example, we talk about religion and politics, we have already assumed they refer to different things, and to mutually incompatible ones at that. Politics is secular, which means non-religious. Religion is separate from politics. If the two get mixed up and confused, then there is a problem.

One thing to notice here is that there has been a massive historical slippage from 'ought' to 'is'. What started in the 17th century as an 'ought' – viz. there *ought to be* a distinction between 'religion' and 'political society' – has long become an assumption about the way the world actually *is*. In public discourse we have become used to talking as if 'religion' and 'politics' refer to two essentially different aspects of the real world, that we intuitively know what a religion is and what politics is, and we imagine that if we wanted to take the trouble we could define their essential differences. And yet of course the rhetorical construct of 'ought' keeps appearing, as for example when we insist that a nation that does not have a constitutional separation of religion and politics is undeveloped or backward; or when Anglican Bishops make moral pronouncements that seem uncomfortably 'political'.

But what does 'politics' actually refer to? If the meaning of a word is to be found in its use, then we surely all know the meaning of 'politics'. We use the term constantly. We have an intuitive understanding about what politics is. If we didn't, how would we be able to deploy the term with such self-assurance? How, without understanding the term, would we be able to communicate about our shared and contested issues? We discourse constantly about politics, whether in private, or in the media, in our schools and universities, or in our 'political' institutions – and we surely all know which of our institutions are the political ones. Careers are made in politics. We join political parties, or we become politicians, or we enrol and study in departments of political science, and read and write textbooks on the topic. How could there be a political science if we did not know what politics is? There are journalists and academics that specialise in politics, journals dedicated to politics, distinct associations and conferences for its study, and thousands of books written and published about politics. Historians research the politics of the past. There is a politics industry. There are commercial companies that analyse and provide data on the topic of politics. Media organisations employ many people to produce programmes dedicated to politics and to political analysis, discussion and debate.

Yet the ubiquity of politics is our problem. For politics and the political is so universal that it is difficult to pin it down. Are there any domains of human living that cannot and are not described as being political, as pertaining to politics?

If we try to find some definitive use of the terms 'politics' and 'political' by searching through popular and academic books, newspapers, TV representations, or the discourses on politics on the internet, it is difficult not to come to the conclusion that everything is politics or political. We can find representations of the politics of abortion, the politics of hunger, church politics, the politics of sectarianism, political Islam, the politics of universities and university departments, the politics of medieval Japan, the politics of the Roman or the Mughal empires, the politics of slavery, class politics, the politics of caste in colonial and contemporary India, the politics of Native Americans in the 16th century, the politics of ancient Babylon, the politics of marriage, the politics of Constitutions, and so on and on. And we surely know that politics is as ancient as the hills.

This apparent universality of the political, its lack of boundaries, seems to place a question mark around its semantic content. If we cannot say what is *not* politics, then how can we give any determinate content or meaning to the term? This lack of boundaries can also be seen in the problem of demarcating a domain of politics from other domains such as 'religion' and 'economics'. If we try to find a clear distinction between politics and religion, we find a history of contestation, but one that only seems to go back to the 17th century – a point to which I return in a moment. We find claims that politics and religion have – or ought to have – nothing to do with each other, yet in contemporary discourse we find many references to the politics of religion, and also to the religion of politics.

The term 'political economy' also points us towards this problem of demarcation. Some universities have departments of politics, some have departments of economics, and some have departments of political economy. How are they distinguished? This is especially perplexing when one finds books written by specialists on the politics of economics, as well as on the economics of politics. Add in works on the religion of politics and the politics of religion; or the religion of economics and the economics of religion: we seem to have a dog's dinner of categories. You notice these things when you read outside your normal disciplinary boundaries. It is also of interest that all of these can and are described as sciences: viz. the science of politics, the science of religion, and the science of economics.

We cannot in practice easily if at all distinguish between the categories on which these putative sciences are based. Yet all of them have their own specialist departments, degree courses, journals, associations and conferences.

Another point is that all these 'sciences', based on concepts so difficult to distinguish and demarcate, are 'secular', in the sense of *non-religious*. Describing a science or discipline as secular reminds us that we have another demarcation problem. If all secular practices and institutions are defined as non-religious and therefore in distinction to 'religion', we need to have some reasonably clear understanding about what we mean by religion to be able to make the distinction in the first place. Without such an understanding, how would we know what 'non-religious' means? This paradox is magnified when we consider that for many centuries 'secular' has referred mainly to the 'secular priesthood' in the Catholic Church, and the priesthood are hardly non-religious in the modern sense.

We thus find that in everyday discussions and debates, and also in the more specialist discourses, we deploy concepts with a largely unquestioned confidence that on further consideration seems unfounded. Speaking personally, I entered academic work through religious studies, also known as the science (or scientific study) of religion, the history of religions, or the plain study of religions. Yet I cannot tell you what religion is, or what the relation between [singular] religion and [plural] religions is. I have made it a point over many years of tracking down a wide range of definitions of religion, and found them to be contradictory and circular. There is no agreed definition of the subject that so many experts claim to be researching and writing about. I suggest this is the situation in politics as well. Attempts that I have read to define politics, for example in text-books written for students of politics, seem always to be circular in the sense that they define politics in terms of political attributes, just as religions are defined in terms of religious attributes.

I suggest that the perceived self-evidence of politics as a meaningful category derives from an inherent ambiguity – and in this it is a mirror-image to religion. On the one hand, the term 'politics' generally simply means 'power' or 'contestations of power', and since power is probably one of the few universals in human relations we can see why it might appear intuitively convincing.

However, on that understanding, it is difficult to see what is *not* about politics, because it can surely be argued that all human relations have always been about contestations of power. We gain such ubiquity at the expense of meaning. Surely, political science has a more specific and determinate meaning than power studies? You might just as well say that the study of politics is the study of humanity.

Our sense that there is a more determinate nuance seems justified when we discover that the discourse on 'politics' has a specific genesis in the English language in the 17th century. Though we can find a few (probably very few) references to 'politicians' in Elizabethan drama, 'politics' is even rarer, and I cannot find a sustained discourse on politics as a distinct domain of human action earlier than John Locke's late 17th century distinctions, developed in his Treatises on Government, between 'man in the state of nature' and 'political society'. Here Locke explicitly distinguishes between man in the state of nature and political or civil society on the one hand; and also between politics and religion on the other. In his religion-politics binary, Locke links politics to the outer, public order of the magistrate and governance, and religion to the inner, private relation of the individual to God. (What he means by 'god' is itself a conundrum, for the evidence is that, like Newton, he was a heretic, either a Unitarian or a Socinian. 'God' is another of those endlessly contested categories. If you try to define 'religion' as 'belief in god', you find yourself in another infinite regress of meanings).

It seems significant that this politics-religion binary is a modern, Enlightenment one, because Locke was arguing *against* the dominant understanding of Religion at the time. For his own reasons he wanted to reimagine 'religion'. When the term religion was used at all (rarer than today) it meant Christian truth, and there was no clear sense (despite Locke's claims) that Christian truth was not about power, or that it was separated from governance.

The King was the sacred head and heart of the Christian Commonwealth, and what fell outside religion in this dominant sense was not a neutral *non-religious* domain but pagan irrationality and barbarity. In other words, what fell outside religion in the dominant sense of his day was still defined theologically and biblically in terms of The Fall. His privatization of religion to make way for a public domain of political society was an ideologically-motivated claim about how we *ought* to think about religion, not a neutral description of some objective facts.

It was especially in his attempt to legitimate new concepts of private property, and the rights of (male) property owners to representation, that Locke needed to completely revise people's understanding of 'religion' as a private affair of the inner man (women were not much in the picture), in order to demarcate an essentially different domain called political society.

This new binary found its way into written constitutions in North America, and is now naturalised in common speech and common sense. Today it seems counter-intuitive to question the reality of politics as a distinct domain of human practice. But this rhetorical construction was deeply resisted. Even the French Revolution did not succeed in formally separating religion and the state until the end of the 19th century. England was an Anglican confessional state until well into the 19th century.

Locke's formulation was thoroughly ideological but has become naturalised through repeated rhetorical construction until now it seems to be 'in the nature of things'. I suggest that, whenever we use the term politics with intuitive ease we catch ourselves and ask, in what sense am I using the term? Am I using it in the universal sense of ubiquitous power and contestations of power in all human relations? Or as referring to a specific ideological formation of modernity underpinning a historically-emergent form of private property-ownership and representation of (male) property interests? The elided slippage between the historically and ideologically specific formulation, and the empty ubiquity of 'power' as a universal in all human relations, lends the term its illusory quality of intuitive common sense.

CRITICAL RELIGION AND ECONOMY

FICTIONS AND CONTENTIONS: CRITICAL RELIGION IN A TIME OF CRISIS

Brian Nail

While Critical Religion scholars demonstrate a range of disciplinary and methodological perspectives, the work of many is characterized by the ability to apply insights from the study of religious cultures and texts to an analysis of the conflicts of an ostensibly modern-secular world. In an age of acute political and social turmoil, when events and texts are increasingly truncated via the decontextualizing force of digital media, there is an urgent need for this sort of scholarly critique. Although the expansion of internet technology has provided hitherto unimaginable access to knowledge and real-time data about our world, we are also living in a time of unrelenting uncertainty.

Economic and statistical data have become the prophetic texts of our time, yet data science has proven mainly incapable of effectively predicting the occurrence of seemingly anomalous events, such as the election of Donald Trump to become president of the United States, Britain's decision to permanently leave the European Union, or the numerous acts of political violence that plague our world. It has been over ten years since the global financial crisis set into motion a worldwide recession.

The financial crisis and its economic and political consequences motivated many to question the stability and legitimacy of the liberal democratic order. This crisis of legitimacy has subsequently reignited the passions of many fundamentalist and racist ideologies while also revealing the unacknowledged violence that has persisted at the heart of so-called civil society. Collectively, these events, combined with the onslaught of numerous climate change induced natural disasters, have brought the fragile state of our shared lifeworld clearly into view.[1]

The crises of our present age are not historically unprecedented, but their scale and intensity have perhaps grown due to the deeply interconnected and yet economically disparate state of human society. An understanding of the dynamics of religion as a social, cultural, and political phenomenon provides a useful methodological approach for understanding the conflicts that have come to define our contemporary world. While the various disciplinary factions of theology and religious studies maintain their own particular, often contradictory, understandings of religion, Critical Religion acknowledges the pluriform nature of the practice and study of religion. As a cultural expression, religion has historically provided humans with a way of understanding the world and their experiences in it. As Gavin Flood observes, "This strange world is always culturally mediated. We experience the world through cultures and systems of signs and symbols that link us to each other, to the past, and to the future."[2] A knowledge of religious semiosis provides crucial insight into the ways that humans form communities and cope with a strange and uncertain world.

The world is, and always has been, an uncertain place. In his homage to the Delta bluesman Charley Patton, Bob Dylan sings, "High water risin', risin' night and day. All the gold and silver are being stolen away. . . . I just can't be happy, love. Unless you're happy too. It's bad out there. High water everywhere."[3] Dylan is borrowing heavily from his source material here. In Patton's "High Water Everywhere," the bluesman documents the catastrophic effects of the Great Mississippi Flood of 1927 for black residents of the Delta, who were deliberately prevented from seeking shelter on higher ground that was reserved for their white neighbors: "Lord, the whole round country, man, it's overflowed. . . . I would go to the hill country

---

[1] Jürgen Habermas. *The Theory of Communicative Action: Reason and the Rationalization of Society*, trans. Thomas McCarthy, vol. 1, 2 (Cambridge: Polity, 1984).
[2] Gavin Flood. *The Importance of Religion: Meaning and Action in Our Strange World* (Oxford: Wiley-Blackwell, 2012), 7.
[3] Bob Dylan. *High Water (For Charley Patton), Love and Theft* (Sony Music, 2001).

but they got me barred."[4] Contrary to the neoliberal discourse of late capitalist modernity, which obscures the human agency underlying financial and environmental catastrophes, the blues is rooted in the political-theological reality of disaster. Racial politics and self-interest, rather than quasi-divine market forces and white myths of personal sin, determine who is abandoned to the flood and who stands ready to benefit in its wake.

Water will rise – money will be scarce or otherwise expropriated. Hope and love are the only reliable but often rare resources for survival. But Patton is conjuring ancient knowledge – this flood imagery is drawn from a synthesis of folk history and biblical myth. The Flood myth in the book of Genesis explicitly thematizes the paradoxical dynamics of creative-destruction that characterize the (re)creation of sociopolitical order in the wake of crisis. However, many of the narrative contradictions of the Flood myth in Genesis are mystified through the superimposition of a certain Christian theological tradition of interpretation that obscures some of the more uniquely human dimensions of the story.

In his commentary on Genesis, Edwin Good suggests that the traditional emphasis upon 'sin' as a justification for the flood has obscured the complex role of the divine within the story. He argues that "theology has not paid attention to ways in which its sacred book suggests that the creator failed the creation, especially by not considering implications of some of his own decisions. Several divine actions seem, on contemplation, to have been less than adequate."[5] This sort of Christian theodicy mystifies the creative-destructive dynamics of the creator by glossing over some of the more problematically human characteristics of the divine. It performs the logic of retroactive justification that we often see deployed in contemporary political discourse. To uncover some the Flood myth's theological and narrative complexities, a comparative reading of one of Genesis's literary counterparts may be illuminating.

Among other crucial insights, a reading of The Epic of Gilgamesh reveals humankind's longstanding awareness of the inevitability of environmental, economic, and political ruin. In the poem, Gilgamesh is heralded as "He who saw the Deep, the country's foundation," and he attains his symbolic power through a series of violent conflicts. Mourning the loss of his beloved

---

[4] David Evans, "High Water Everywhere: Blues and Gospel Commentary on the 1927 Mississippi River Flood," in *Nobody Knows Where the Blues Come from: Lyrics and History*, ed. Robert Springer (Jackson: University Press of Mississippi, 2007), 60–63.

[5] Edwin Good. *Genesis 1-11: Tales of the Earliest World* (Stanford: Stanford University Press, 2011), 76.

Enkidu, Gilgamesh goes in search of Utnapishtim to find the secret to eternal life. The Flood myth – the primordial crisis narrative – is presented as Utnapishtim conveys the story of how he and his family survived the great flood. The Flood myth is itself a parable of sovereignty. It is a story about the creative-destruction of sociopolitical order.

After the flood, the gods must re-establish civilization, and, according to Andrew George, that order is somehow divinely contiguous with that which existed before it – "This was important, for the traditional belief was that the gods had supplied all that was needed for human beings to flourish – cities, agriculture, the arts of civilization – at the outset of human history, in the antediluvian age. Nothing more was to be discovered; the antediluvian model was how human society should be run."[6] The narrative contours of this myth – the anthropocentric tale of a "survivable apocalypse"[7] and the notion that the sovereign alone possesses the knowledge and wisdom to re-establish a utopian existence that is purely imaginary – continue to operate in every appeal to "make America great again" and the unrealized project of restoring to Britain its illusion of sovereignty.

The Flood myth reveals an insoluble link between creation and destruction, life and death, that defies the modern logic of crisis – which is structured according to the Enlightenment myth of time as the uninterrupted march of progress. As part of an oral literary tradition, the telling of such stories itself is an act of creative-destruction: the cultural knowledge and theological perspectives presented through the poems connect listeners with the narratives of preceding generations, connecting them to a cultural imaginary centuries in the making, while also adapting those stories to suit the needs and circumstances of a new generation. It is an exercise in preservation as well as improvisation.[8] The narrative forms that have been designed to address the uncertainty of life in late capitalist modernity retain the creative-destructive character of ancient crisis myths. However, their fictional and perhaps even theological dimensions are mystified.

During Alan Greenspan's testimony before the U.S. Congress in the wake of 2008 financial crisis, the former chair of the Federal Reserve was asked whether or not his ideological commitment to the self-correcting nature of

---

[6] *The Epic of Gilgamesh: A New Translation* (London: Penguin, 2000), xlix.
[7] Samuel Tongue. "'It's Not the End of the World': Aronofsky's Noah and IMAXed Apocalyptic Animals," in *Noah as Antihero: Darren Aronofsky's Cinematic Deluge*, ed. Rhonda Burnette-Bletsch and Jon Morgan (London: Routledge, 2017), 183–98.
[8] Walter J. Ong. *Orality and Literacy: The Technologizing of the Word* (London; New York: Routledge, 1982).

the free market prevented him from taking measures to curb irresponsible lending practices.

Greenspan replied, "Well, remember that what an ideology is, is a conceptual framework with the way people deal with reality. Everyone has one. You have to – to exist, you need an ideology. The question is whether it is accurate or not. And what I'm saying to you is, yes, I found a flaw. I don't know how significant or permanent it is, but I've been very distressed by that fact."[9] Greenspan confessed that he had underestimated the extent to which self-interested financiers would be willing to provide high-risk loans that would ultimately threaten to undermine the very industry of corporate finance itself. He had placed too much trust in the myth of the self-correcting free market, a myth that remains a cornerstone of classical economic theory. His response reveals what is at risk when we obscure or otherwise disregard the link between our socioeconomic and political reality and the myths that found it.

The epistemological assumptions of economic theory are inextricably linked with contemporary political discourse, particularly within the current neoliberal era. The economic historian Mary S. Morgan argues that economic theory is primarily a modelling science that relies upon visual and literary representations of the world which are essentially fictional. Although the curved lines in a classic econometric diagram of supply and demand may be based upon personal experiences of purchasing and some casual observation of market behaviours, the lines of course do not reflect actual observations of supply and demand because such invisible phenomena are not there to be seen in the world.

There is, therefore, a double-layer of imagination reflected in these diagrams which reflects the highly speculative and fictional nature of economic modelling. According to Morgan, the answer to the question, "How do economists use models? is, in one sense, easy to answer: they ask questions with them and tell stories! Or more exactly: they ask questions, use the resources of the model to demonstrate something, and tell stories in the process."[10] The narrative power of these fictive models enables them to function as epistemic instruments which represent the world to the minds of

---

[9] "Greenspan Admits 'Flaw' to Congress, Predicts More Economic Problems," *PBS NewsHour* (blog), accessed July 9, 2014, http://www.pbs.org/newshour/bb/business-july-dec08-crisishearing_10-23/.

[10] Mary S. Morgan. *The World in the Model: How Economists Work and Think* (Cambridge: Cambridge University Press, 2012), 217–18.

those who rely upon them for evaluating and predicting behaviour in the so-called "real world."

There is a striking similarity between the way that Morgan describes the hermeneutic operations which characterize the ways that economists interpret their models and the notion of the self-interpreting bible which emerged during the time of the Reformation. When economists read their own diagrams, they entertain the illusion of self-mastery and self-presencing that accompanies the experience of reading an all too human text that has nonetheless been imbued with divine powers. Although such texts appear to be epistemologically and ontologically stable according to a certain scientific outlook, they are nonetheless fictional and continue to possess the creative-destructive dynamics associated with other more ancient narrative forms designed to anticipate and respond to our crisis-prone world. However, unlike the narratives of an oral literary tradition, which are shaped and moulded to meet the everchanging expectations of their audience, the founding myths of capitalist modernity, and most importantly the economic clerics who maintain them, demand unwavering fidelity to tradition.

The fact that the narrative abstractions of ancient and modern myths each have a tendency to disguise or otherwise disregard the complexities of human life is of course not a new insight for those working in fields which take seriously the particularity of human subjectivity. And for scholars working in the broad field of Critical Religion, this has meant contending with a great number of dogmas and philosophical traditions, inside of as well as outwith our respective disciplines, which have historically sacrificed the irreducible complexity of human life for the sake of elaborating highly debatable answers to life's most perplexing questions. It is not coincidental that the field of Critical Religion has emerged during a time of religious as well as economic crisis. In the midst of crisis, there is a certain urgency that stimulates new modes of critique. The challenge, of course, is that like Utnapishtim, scholars must somehow survive the flood to the tell the tale.

Works Cited

Dylan, Bob. *High Water (For Charley Patton). Love and Theft*. Sony Music, 2001.

Evans, David. "High Water Everywhere: Blues and Gospel Commentary on the 1927 Mississippi River Flood." In *Nobody Knows Where the Blues Come from: Lyrics and History*, edited by Robert Springer, 3–75. Jackson: University Press of Mississippi, 2007.

Flood, Gavin D. *The Importance of Religion: Meaning and Action in Our Strange World*. Oxford: Wiley-Blackwell, 2012.

George, Andrew. *The Epic of Gilgamesh: A New Translation*. London: Penguin, 2000.

Good, Edwin. *Genesis 1-11: Tales of the Earliest World*. Stanford: Stanford University Press, 2011.

"Greenspan Admits 'Flaw' to Congress, Predicts More Economic Problems." PBS NewsHour (blog). Accessed July 9, 2014. http://www.pbs.org/newshour/bb/business-july-dec08-crisishearing_10-23/.

Habermas, Jürgen. *The Theory of Communicative Action: Reason and the Rationalization of Society*. Translated by Thomas McCarthy. Vol. 1. 2. Cambridge: Polity, 1984.

Morgan, Mary S. *The World in the Model: How Economists Work and Think*. Cambridge: Cambridge University Press, 2012.

Ong, Walter J. Orality and Literacy: *The Technologizing of the Word*. London; New York: Routledge, 1982.

Tongue, Samuel. "'It's Not the End of the World': Aronofsky's Noah and IMAXed Apocalyptic Animals." In *Noah as Antihero: Darren Aronofsky's Cinematic Deluge*, edited by Rhonda Burnette-Bletsch and Jon Morgan, 183–98. London: Routledge, 2017.

"PROFITS OF DOOM"

Andrew W. Hass

"The governments don't rule the world; Goldman Sachs rules the world."

– Alessio Rastani[1]

There have always been prophets of doom. History is punctuated by exclamatory voices crying, in one form or other, that catastrophe is imminent or the end is nigh. These voices often pronounce their message in the name of some divine authority, whether the Hebrew prophets, who spoke on behalf of Yahweh, the Greek Sibyls, who spoke as ones possessed by Zeus and the gods, or the first Christian prophet, who audaciously claimed, or at the very least insinuated, he *was* God. Subsequent doomsayers have varied, yet most all have grounded their proclamations on some otherworldly source, even if these are of an astrological, astronomical, or occultic nature. There are limits, however: few have prophesied an alien invasion, for

---

[1] "'Anyone can make money from a crash,' says market trader", *BBC Online*, last accessed June 10, 2020, https://www.bbc.co.uk/news/av/business-15059135/anyone-can-make-money-from-a-crash-says-market-trader.

example, simply because the doom, to be taken with any degree of seriousness, must seem plausible within our immediate context. The signs must be ripe – as signs of our times. (How can you predict, much less give credibility to, *alien* times?)

So it was that as I listened years ago to one of the latest prophets of doom to emerge, and who at the time went, as they now say, "viral", I was struck by the utter disconnect from any divine or other-worldly authority. Today's messengers of doom no longer need divine underwriting, because humankind has advanced to a point where, in the last century, it has become capable of destroying the entire world completely by its own devices. This is not just imminent doom; it is now, and entirely, immanent doom. Typical to our world, the latest prophets also carry no sustaining effect. They are five-minute prophets, fame-mongers with proclamations designed for the transience of the headline, the ephemerality of the sound-bite. In this sense they are seldom real prophets by any proper definition. What also struck me in this case, however, was that, though none had heard of his name before, and few have heard of his name since, and though he was clearly and unashamedly out for his micro-minute of fame, his message was able to plunge deep below the surface of ubiquitous political, social, and economic gloom, into the subterranean depths of *immanent* doom.

The doom I'm speaking about issued from a BBC interview of an independent stock market trader Alessio Rastani, who, even in his own industry, was relatively unknown.[2] His notoriety rose dramatically when, asked for a television on-air interview, as an expert in the trading world, to comment on the state of the world markets, and the Eurozone markets in particular, he held nothing back. The markets *will crash*, he exclaimed, without any prelude or fanfare, because "markets right now are ruled by fear". We've all heard such prognostications before, and, quite frankly, few of us would take this seriously, because we all know the markets are virtually impossible to predict with any accuracy. But this claim, in a long line of many just like it, was not the source of the doom. It was rather what he admitted shortly afterwards: "personally, I've been dreaming of this moment for three years." Here was the predatory trader acknowledging that market economies and market stability are not his, nor any of his colleagues, concern. He just wants to make money, and if a market crash can make him money – in his eyes, a ton of money – then it cannot come soon enough.

---

[2] Ibid.

This brought to my mind Walter Benjamin's famous fragment "Capitalism as Religion", in which he claims that capitalism holds a similar structure to religion, with four distinguishing characteristics: 1) it holds to no special dogma or theology; 2) it is ceaseless, with no ritualised sense of time (no Sabbath, no sacred holidays); 3) it is wholly guilt-ridden, rather than repentance based; and 4) it necessarily conceals its God.[3] Now much has been made of these nascent thoughts of Benjamin, and increasingly much justification has been found for them. Few today would contest the ceaseless nature of capitalist forces, or that its dogma, if it has any, is, like its God, concealed amid the worldliness of its operations. Economies are wholly human affairs, and the attainment of wealth through capitalist mechanisms, capitalist strategies, and capitalist motivations buries any religious faith and fervour well enough below the surface of its gross materialism. But occasionally a deep rumbling within – implosive bank greed, or wild market volatility that follows upon disruptive events – shows up the tenuous nature of its belief system, and the "cultic" nature of its structure (Benjamin's term) begins to suggest a different level of operation. And one simply needs to reflect upon the motto written on all American paper money to see that the connection is, as Benjamin had seen already in the early 1920s, more than suggestive: "In God We Trust". (Benjamin went even further, and compared the human images on banknotes to iconography.)

But the third characteristic, Benjamin's notion of guilt, has always been the most difficult to ascertain. Benjamin claims that the cult of capitalism engenders blame, that an "enormous feeling of guilt not itself knowing how to repent, grasps at the cult".[4] Yet the statement remains oblique, and the author never elaborates just what this guilt is for, and why it might include God Himself in its comprehensive power. We are left, from the fragment, to supply our own reasoning: the guilt of profit for its own sake, perhaps, or in more Marxian terms, the guilt of alienation or of the exploitation of the labourer.

As I listened to Rastani, who was simply a momentary spokesman for the trading industry at its most voracious, the industry that brought a global fiscal meltdown through the sub-prime market in 2008, and against which various movements have tried to resist unsuccessfully, I began to wonder if Benjamin had got this point about guilt correct. The revelation here was the

---

[3] Walter Benjamin. "Capitalism as Religion", trans. Chad Kautzer, in *The Frankfurt School on Religion*, ed. Eduardo Mendieta (New York: Routledge, 2005), pp. 259-260.
[4] Ibid. p. 259.

very absence of any guilt. What left the interviewer's mouth gaping was the vulture-like indifference to the suffering of the wounded animal. Or perhaps indifference is too kind – the rapacity. Guilt was not only missing; it was not part of this trader's genetic code.

But there may be another way to read Benjamin on this point. The German word for guilt that Benjamin has used here is *Schuld*, which has two further related meanings: blame and debt. It is thus not simply that capitalism engenders culpability in either exploiting or being exploited; it is also that the system places us all in a position of unmitigated debt. And this is not merely financial debt, though for many, and increasingly, it may be all too financial. Like most religions, it involves a perpetual owing, a being on credit to the system (the gods/God), but now without ever a payment to come, or goods to be exchanged (exoneration, atonement, reconciliation, redemption). What Rastani, this momentary prophet of doom, betrays for us is that we lie in wait for a catastrophe that, whether it comes or not, never allows us to get outside the system that generates it. For if the market crashes, most of us are in debt for what we cannot pay. But the few who make money are also in debt, and at a more profound level – to the system that profited for them. They don't make the money directly themselves; they are indebted to the system to do this. (Money, we remember, has only ever been a token for what we have made. Commodities trading is only ever the exchange of tokens for what has been traded, money – even further removed from reality.) We are all in debt to a system, to an economy of intangible forces, that we have no way to transcend, since what we've gained is itself the means for gaining it. As someone has astutely said of capitalism's circularity, "Everything that has meaning is immediately identical with *what it means*".[5]

Our prophet in three years waiting is himself doomed, not because he may never strike it rich – enough in his industry clearly have – but because by striking it rich, he will, of necessity, be swallowed up in the despair of not being able to redeem himself, or of not being able to convert the material back into anything other than the material. Thus, as Benjamin says, all we attain is a "world of despair".[6]

Now the conversion of money back into material goods is precisely what any profit-seeker ultimately hopes for, since with material prosperity comes,

---

[5] Werner Hamacher. "Guilt History: Benjamin's Sketch 'Capitalism as Religion'", trans. Kirk Wetters, in *Diacritics*, 32, no. 3-4 (Fall-Winter 2002), 87.
[6] Benjamin. *Capitalism as Religion*, 260.

the cult of the system tells us, peace of mind, self-direction, and the so-called good life. Yet every other religion, including even the ancient Epicureans, has taught the opposite: money does not bring happiness. This is a stock piece of wisdom. Why is it that the religion of capitalism has had such a difficult time understanding such a basic, and we might even now say, superficial teaching? Perhaps we can now answer: guilt – to abandon its God, Mammon, the concealed God of self-generating abstracted profit, or the commodification of money for its own internal sake, and not for the sake of the very self that is in despair, is to foreclose on the debt we owe it. But with such a guilt comes the very obliteration of our being, individual and collective.[7] Such is the doom that awaits us.

That no one has yet found an alternative to this religion and its guilt, and least of all the religions of the West that have become synonymous with them – this is what is truly despairing. Even such push-back as the Occupy movements could not sustain a countering force. There seems nothing on the horizon to disenfranchise capitalism in the form that we have come to know it. This will only happen, I expect, when a counterforce sees and addresses the religious nature of the system, and addresses the immanent guilt and debt at its core.

---

[7] Ibid.: "Therein lies the historical enormity of capitalism: religion is no longer the reform of being, but rather its obliteration."

Works Cited

"'Anyone can make money from a crash,' says market trader". *BBC Online*. Last accessed June 10, 2020. https://www.bbc.co.uk/news/av/business-15059135/anyone-can-make-money-from-a-crash-says-market-trader.

Benjamin, Walter. "Capitalism as Religion", trans. Chad Kautzer, in *The Frankfurt School on Religion*, ed. Eduardo Mendieta (New York: Routledge, 2005), pp. 259-260.

Hamacher, Werner. "Guilt History: Benjamin's Sketch 'Capitalism as Religion'", trans. Kirk Wetters, in *Diacritics*, 32, no. 3-4 (Fall-Winter 2002): 81-106.

POSTMODERNISM, POSTCOLONIALISM, AND THE PRIVATE PROPERTY SOCIETY

Timothy Fitzgerald

'Religion' is part of a classification system that appears to the secular liberal as neutral, given unproblematically in consciousness as corresponding to how the world is, independent of the discursive formations that constitute our collective inter-subjective apprehensions. Yet on the contrary, classification systems embody power relations. Critical religion proposes that religion is a power category that, in dialectical interplay with other power categories such as 'politics', 'science' or 'nature', constructs a world and our own apprehensions according to the interests of private property, and the various beliefs, institutions and practices that have come into the world to protect private property.[1]

The right to the outright private ownership of the earth, including the right to buy and sell for purely personal gain, unencumbered by any effects the practice might have on the lives of other people or the environment, is a historically peculiar idea, one which would have been incomprehensible to most of the peoples who ever existed.[2] And yet this masculinist fiction of the naturally possessive individual and his supposed rights of private ownership

---

[1] Timothy Fitzgerald. *Religion and Politics in International Relations: The Modern Myth*, (London: Bloomsbury, 2011).

[2] See Andro Linklater. *Owning the Earth: The Transforming History of Land Ownership* (London: Bloomsbury, 2013).

– rights for which women had to struggle for centuries to achieve for themselves – has been transformed into our dominant notion of 'human nature', and has become the globalising norm of the world order.

The category religion has a unique function in the way it enables the mythical basis of private ownership of the earth, and makes it seem normal and inevitable. The right to unlimited private accumulation of our common organic inheritance, regardless of the effect on the rest, is the default position of liberal and neoliberal capitalism. In putative contrast to the blind faith of 'believers', private ownership of the earth is celebrated by generations of secular liberals as an enlightened discovery, a sign of a higher stage of progress and development, our collective arrival at mature knowledge of 'reality', including what it means to be human.

Critical religion is a revolutionary practice that seeks to subvert the rhetorical illusions that transform a peculiar way of owning the earth into common sense normality, as though there is an inherent inevitability – betrayed by such common expressions as "that's the way the world is", "you can't change human nature", or "stuff happens" – that the land, the air, the water, the energy, and even the genes of our collective organic inheritance can be privately owned and privately profited from, with minimal if any responsibility for impact on the remainder.

It follows from this position that there cannot be a genuine postmodern or postcolonial consciousness at least until the modern liberal categories of the understanding have been critically deconstructed and the illusion that they are neutral and objective has been dispelled. To be postmodern and postcolonial is to be post the categories of secular liberal understanding. We are not there yet.

To faithfully pursue this process brings one up against the inflexible resistance of the liberal or neoliberal university and its structures and priorities. This critical challenge to the dominant norms does not win one many friends. The liberal universities within which we work reflect and reproduce these ideological priorities. This is a good reason why liberal academics cannot effectively stand up against the neoliberal transformation of universities into business corporations with top-down, anti-democratic managerial structures, and an obsessive reduction of all values to market commodities.

Works Cited

Fitzgerald, Timothy. *Religion and Politics in International Relations: The Modern Myth.* London: Bloomsbury, 2011.

Linklater, Andro. *Owning the Earth: The Transforming History of Land Ownership.* London: Bloomsbury, 2013.

CRITICAL RELIGION, GENDER AND SEXUALITY

CRITICAL RELIGION AND FEMALE GENIUS

Alison Jasper

Part of the rationale for critical religion is that it helps make clear how the terms 'religious' and 'religion,' frame and perpetuate colonial or western-centred attitudes and assumptions. I argue that these attitudes and assumptions connect with concepts of gender. In other words, I suggest, there is an underlying alignment between the 'religion/secular' binary and the historical desire of Protestant Christianity to establish its exclusive claim to the former term, and a continuing normative western desire to sustain the considerable privileges associated with the male term in a male/female binary. Mirroring and rationalising this pattern of gendered hierarchical power, symbols of western Protestant Christianity have been translated across the modern world through wide ranging colonial – including missionary - activity. Where this pattern is promoted, practices and attitudes, now more widely viewed as inequitable, are still justified through reference to divine power or authority.

In this context, the binary distinction between 'religion' and 'the secular' – as critically dissected in discussions of 'critical religion' – has been seen as useful to some – including some feminists. Making a distinction between 'secular' reason and powerful 'religious' – i.e. immature and arbitrary (Immanuel Kant, 'An Answer to the Question: What is Enlightenment?', 1784) or violently hegemonic (Samuel Huntington, The Clash of Civilisations and the Remaking of World Order, 1996) – justifications of male authority, has, some say, allowed women to identify themselves with the former. Identifying themselves with the possibilities of a rational and critical process (the process that arguably also helped produce this distinction at the beginning of the European Enlightenment) there is some chance of proving themselves the equal of men.

In response I would say first that forms of hegemony are resilient. Even when the idea of female blameworthiness and moral inferiority – expressed powerfully in the Biblical story of how Eve led Adam into sin – began to lose its hold on the popular imagination in the 19th century, and in spite of the Enlightenment, other ways to challenge women's access to equitable forms of freedom, respect and opportunity have continued to pop up! Attempts to essentialise 'women' as inherently incapable of excelling, as sinful or in some kind of 'natural' sense either fitted or unfit, have been emerging probably as long as patriarchal societies have existed and thus not all of them in relation to the forms and symbols of Christianity. In this sense, a critical approach is clearly a desirable tool for a woman to have and use – whether or not a man first gave it his name! But it is not a panacea. Secondly of course, if critical religion aims to present a critique of the religion/secular binary itself, it should for these reasons remember always also to keep gendered binaries in its critical sights.

Works Cited

Huntington, Samuel P. *The Clash of Civilisations and the Remaking of World Order*. New York: Simon & Schuster, 1996.

Kant, Immanuel. *An Answer to the Question: What is Enlightenment? (1784)*. Translated by H. B. Nisbet. New York: Penguin Press, 2009.

THE BIBLE AND HOMOSEXUALITY

Alison Jasper

A few years ago, I came across a book that I thought shed some useful light on the issue of homosexuality from a Hebrew Bible perspective. The book was *The Bible Now: Homosexuality, Abortion, Women, Death Penalty, Earth* by Richard Friedman and Shawna Dolansky. In fairly short space it sets out a summary of most of the major arguments about specific Biblical references to homosexuality in the Hebrew Bible, those Jewish scriptures with which the Christian Old Testament overlaps to a considerable extent.

Firstly they are very clear that the law in the Biblical book of Leviticus (notably, Lev 18:22 and Lev 20:13) cannot simply be wished away.[1] So for those who regard the Hebrew Bible as their rule book, the prohibition on (male) homosexual behaviour in the Hebrew Bible has to be addressed. But at the same time, Friedman and Dolansky argue that we cannot ignore the context of these references either. It is a very different context to that of most contemporary western readers.

---

[1] Richard Friedman and Shawna Dolansky. *The Bible Now: Homosexuality, Abortion, Women, Death Penalty, Earth* (Oxford: Oxford University Press, 2011), 26.

For one thing, people in the ancient near east did not make the distinction between homosexuality and heterosexuality as if it were a distinction between equal concepts. Heterosexuality was the norm across all these cultures. Homosexuality was not – as it is today in many parts of the world – a life-style choice or a marker of individual identity. What these biblical prohibitions on homosexual behaviour seem to reflect in fact, is a widespread construction of sexual relations as relations of power; sexual encounters position each partner hierarchically according to whether their role is active or passive. So, for example, women are suitable sexual partners for men because their active domination by men has already been mystified in terms of their essentially inferior 'nature'. For the same reason, Friedman and Dolansky suggest, some encounters between men have also been socially condoned by association with this active/passive polarity.

The form of socially sanctioned homosexuality we know most about in the Western world – pederastia(boy-love) – existed as a more or less formalised system in Athenian society in the 6th to the 4th centuries BCE[2]. In this case, an older aristocratic male would court a young man of good family "much in the way a man might court a future wife",[3] becoming his mentor and teacher, drawn by an attraction that was erotically charged even if not always acted upon. But tellingly, according to Plato (Symposium, 8,21), the young man – the eromenos – while respectful of his mentor – the erastes – was supposed to remain detached from his sexual passion. And once he reached adulthood and became his social equal, any continuation of a (passive/feminine) sexual relationship became shameful. In a similar way, Friedman and Dolansky look at references to homosexual acts between men in a number of other near eastern contexts containing similar associations between social status and sexual acts between men. (It is also interesting that Friedman and Dolansky insist that there is no prohibition on female homosexual acts in the Hebrew Bible.)

In other words, homosexuality, before the modern era, was always framed by considerations of social status and this forms the wider cultural background to the prohibitions on male homosexuality in the Hebrew Bible and the Christian Old Testament.

However there is also an important difference; male homosexuality is absolutely prohibited in Leviticus 18 and 20. Friedman and Dolansky suggest that this has to do with the fact that the legislative text of which

---

[2] Friedman and Dolansky. *The Bible Now,* 32.
[3] Ibid, 33.

these prohibitions form a part - the Holiness Code[4] – reflects a particular theology of the land. All the people who settle on God's land, both Israelites and aliens, are bound by its ritual and moral law: "In the Holiness Code, there can be no homosexual acts at all in Israel, since by cross-cultural perception such intercourse would necessarily denigrate the passive partner and violate his equal status under God's law".[5] Even the servant and the foreigner in Israel are equal in God's land. And, of course, it remains the case that what is seen as immoral in homosexual acts between men is not the nature of male homosexual desire in itself, but the potential violation of a social equal – an act that would pollute God's land.[6]

In relation to the issue of homosexuality, the authors of *The Bible Now*, come down fairly and squarely in favour of reading the biblical text carefully and in line with principles of critical biblical scholarship. These principles are derived from the so-called 'higher criticism' developed first by European, principally German, University scholarship in the eighteenth and nineteenth centuries. These principles have formed the basis of most western biblical scholarly interpretation since then – whether it is Jewish, Roman Catholic or Protestant. In other words, they are concerned with scientific approaches to history – what here is mythology and what can be cross checked with other evidence and source material from the same period and region. They take due care to learn and understand the original languages of the Bible so they can answer the question, what did the words mean in the original context and how does that differ from the translation?

They discuss the genre and style of writing, conscientiously distinguishing, for example, between poetry, prose and law: "It is one thing to tell a story about something. It is another to write a poem about it. And it is a very different thing to write a law that says 'Thou shalt not do it!'" (p. 1). And finally, they recognise that all readers come to the text with an agenda: a desire to know God's truth or to find the basis of a moral norm or to reveal the gendered, colonialist assumptions of previous readers.

No reading is neutral; hermeneutics or the interpretation of scripture must scrupulously attend to the who, when and where of all readers and authors. This useful treatment of homosexuality in the Hebrew Bible ends on a timely note of caution "Our purpose is not to talk you into one side or the other in these matters. Our purpose is to reveal that this is not a matter for

---

[4] Ibid. 34.
[5] Ibid. 35.
[6] Ibid.

amateurs, and it is not easy. You cannot just open a Bible – especially in translation – and find an obvious answer."[7]

This brings us back to the idea of critical religion. What underpins the rationale for Friedman and Dolansky's book, is a view that opposition to homosexuality today is based on purely subjective considerations and typically couched in the discourse of 'religion' (that is frequently rendered, reductively as 'not the secular') which, in a western context, is more often than not identified with either Islam or a curious entity called Judaeo-Christianity and its scriptures. However, what is disguised in this way is that those who object to the free expression of homosexuality are not sequestered within a single context identified or constrained within the discourse of 'religion'. There are multiple causes for hate speech and homophobia as for sexism and misogyny. The danger is that by associating (opposition to) homosexuality exclusively with 'religion' we allow it either to be dismissed as the expression of a vestigial (declining and not very dangerous) power, or to fuel further distrust of anything operating outside the public, so-called secular (masculine) domain. The religion/secular binary operates unhelpfully in both cases.

---

[7] Ibid. 39.

Works Cited

Friedman, Richard and Dolansky, Shawna. *The Bible Now: Homosexuality, Abortion, Women, Death Penalty, Earth.* Oxford: Oxford University Press, 2011.

PERFORMING GENDER AND SEXUALITY IN EARLY 20TH CENTURY INDIA

Rajalakshmi Nadadur Kannan

Contemporary understandings of Karnatic Music and Bharatnatyam (also known as Indian classical music and dance, respectively) as 'religious' arts that represent Hinduism and Indian culture originated within a very specific historical context: the Indian nationalist movement in the 1920s colonial city of Madras; Partha Chatterjee, discussing a similar movement in Bengal, describes this as 'Classicization'.[1] The nationalist movement in Madras was a 'culture-defining' project in which music and dance were carefully reconstructed by pruning specific practices and traditions to represent the 'pure' inner sphere of spirituality that would displace the outer sphere of colonial politics. Such re-defining of performance arts mystified music and dance performances as 'religious' (read: Hindu) experiences and gendered the performances by defining femininity within the politics of nationalism.

According to this emerging nationalistic patriarchy, whilst the outer/'material' world belonged to men, the inner/'spiritual' world 'assigned' to women had to be protected and nurtured. The nationalist

---

[1] Partha Chatterjee. *The Nation and Its Fragments Colonial and Postcolonial Histories* (Princeton: University Press, 1993), 73.

politics created a new hyper-feminine middle-class woman defined by monogamous conjugal relationships as the Hindu way of life. This woman was defined by her sexual propriety who, through her spirituality, had to maintain the cohesion of family life whilst the man succumbed to the pressures of the material world.

Discourses on women's sexual propriety as a pivotal point of redefining performance arts specifically targeted communities traditionally performing music and dance, the devadāsis. Devadāsi (literally: 'Servant of God') referred to diverse categories of women (and occasionally men) who learned and performed dance and music within diverse settings such as temples or royal courts, festivals and private ceremonies for their patrons. They lived in a matrilineal set-up within a patriarchal society in which they had the right to education and property and enjoyed a high societal status as *nityasumangali* (eternally auspicious). However, in the early 20th century discourses on 'purifying' performance arts focused on two aspects of their tradition: a) they were not bound by monogamous conjugal arrangements; these courtesans went through dedication rituals after which they entered concubinage of the king or became mistresses of their patrons; b) traditionally they performed (among others) compositions that were erotic poems portraying explicit sexual acts (usually between the hero and heroine of the poem/story).

A focus on the devadāsi community, which had a historically significant presence in South India, as a symbol of immorality emerged due to a set of historical developments beginning in the mid-19th century. As court patronages diminished devadāsis moved to Madras and set up salon performances for the newly urbanized audiences, both native and European. The mid-19th century saw transformations in colonial representations of devadāsis from performers of arts (from a tradition outside of monogamous conjugal relationships) to 'prostitutes' who could perform dance and music. This description, 'prostitutes', was affirmed by a series of Anglo-Indian laws passed during the late 19th century modeled after Britain's Contagious Diseases Act that targeted 'prostitutes' catering to British soldiers, and brought devadāsis under the laws.

Judicial definitions, coupled with the influence of the Purity Campaign in 1880s Britain, triggered a politics of morality that resulted in a 'devadāsi-reform' movement, which saw devadāsis as moral deviants from whom sacred music and dance had to be rescued. The early 20th century focus on nationalism and Hinduism, in addition to transforming perceptions of devadāsis, resulted in the movement that defined female sexuality in the public sphere by drawing distinctions between the divine and the erotic. Thus, not only was the divine redefined to indicate a nostalgic pure religious and Hindu past, but the erotic was also redefined as sexual impropriety. Reformers petitioned the government to abolish the devadāsi tradition; the movement was spearheaded by Dr. Muthulakshmi Reddy, who was born into a devadāsi family but rejected the tradition. Her movement received support from (among others) the theosophist Annie Besant and Gandhi, who argued that music and dance were sacred but had been despoiled by devadāsis who had to be rehabilitated to become respectable middle-class women bound and defined by their monogamous conjugal relationships. Despite opposition from the devadāsi community, the Devadāsi Abolition Act was passed in 1947. Devadāsis were thus banned from performing dance and music within a salon set-up.

Whilst the vacuum in the performance space left by devadāsis was being filled by middle-class Brahmin women encouraged by nationalists and organizations such as the Madras Music Academy, these spaces were also being deified. Specifically, Rukmini Devi Arundale, a prominent theosophist and protégé of Annie Besant, employed stagecraft that reified Bharatnatyam as 'religious dance' by conducting a series of performances where she incorporated chants of Sanskrit verses and displayed an icon of Natarāja, an incarnation of the god Shiva in his form as a cosmic dancer, thereby representing the cosmic connection between art and the divine. She introduced sets of compositions in her performances that extolled Natarāja. While the devadāsi repertoire was removed from temple settings, Arundale adopted temple settings to her performance stage through portable temple background sets, thereby deifying the performance space. In contemporary Bharatnatyam performances, the presence of Natarāja idols and temple-setting backgrounds are ubiquitous.

The history of Karnatic Music and Bharatnatyam posits a focus on (among other issues) questions of embodiment and the female body. That the female body is impure had been established in the case of devadāsis within the politics of nationalism: music and dance representing the divine, their 'sacred' (read: 'Hindu') past therefore had to remain 'pure'.

The dimension of embodiment of music and dance permitted by patriarchy represents a dichotomy between the soul and the body in which the soul is the pure inner sphere that connects the performer to the divine, whilst the body represents the material outer sphere that needs to be removed from the context. Women as custodians of this inner spiritual sphere were to learn and perform these arts, thus embodying them, but had to remove the erotic from their performances, which were seen as belonging to the sacred inner space. This solidified the understanding that 'true religion' was sacred and must be distinguished from the non-sacred.

Works Cited

Chatterjee, Partha. *The Nation and Its Fragments Colonial and Postcolonial Histories*. Princeton: University Press, 1993.

AN ARGUMENT FOR THINKING OF RELIGIONS AS VESTIGIAL STATES

Naomi Goldenberg

My hypothesis is that religions can be productively thought of as vestigial states. I consider this to be one way of de-essentializing, demystifying and deconstructing the category of religion. In general, the concept directs theory along two trajectories: one is the analysis of particular histories in which 'religions' are formed or solidified in distinction to 'states'; another is a focus on classifications which current governments use to delineate spheres of power. I understand that if the term vestigial state has any resonance, that it will be as a temporary, partial and provisional tool for building theory in critical religion.

My work draws on James Crawford's discussion of what defines a state in the latest edition of *The Creation of States in International Law*.[1] Although not without its critics, Crawford's articulation of the contingencies attached to the idea of a 'state' remains an important touchstone in international law.

I also refer to texts by Max Weber and Louis Althusser to make my argument that the control of violence is a basic tipping point between what I want to call a vestigial state and a fully empowered government.

---

[1] James Crawford. *The Creation of States in International Law* (Oxford: Oxford University Press, 2006).

Vestigial states tend to behave as once and future states. They are always somewhat restive and are generally eager to take on whatever social, cultural and/or managerial functions the recognized state cedes to them. For example, presently in contemporary nation states, categories of custom and law pertaining to the 'family' are considered proper spheres for 'religious' authority. In contrast, economic policies and most forms of violence are currently placed outside of religious control. Nevertheless, in some jurisdictions 'domestic' violence done in the name of religious practice is tolerated at times. In general, whenever religions, i.e. vestigial states, claim rights in regard to police or military action, they risk being delegitimated in relation to the category of religion. Thus, in regard to Islam, for example, terms such as 'political Islam' or 'Islamist' are invented to cordon off appropriate forms of Islam from those that contemporary nation-states consider inappropriate. I argue that Islam is in the process of being turned into a 'religion' – i.e. of being made 'vestigial' – within some contemporary nation states at the same time that it functions non-vestigially in other parts of the world. Debates about Islam illustrate how 'religion' as a discursive category is employed as a means of control in Western democracies.

My hope is that scholars who specialize in particular historical periods and geographical regions might find the concept of vestigial state to be useful in a range of contexts. I have a particular interest in the shrewd initiative by the Dalai Lama to separate his 'political' functions from his 'religious' ones by encouraging the democratic election of a political leader of the Tibetan people. Thus is Tibetan Buddhism being constructed to conform ever more coherently with the category of 'religion' as a way of limiting the powers of future Dalai Lamas whom China will try to name and control. In my terms, the Dalai Lama is defining himself as a leader of a vestigial state in order to create a separate sphere of 'political' leadership that might escape Chinese influence.

The hypothesis that religions be thought of as vestigial states works well when applied to Jewish history in a manner consonant with the work of Daniel Boyarin in *Border Lines: The Partition of Judaeo-Christianity*[1] and Seth Schwartz in *Imperialism and Jewish Society 200 B.C.E. to 640 C.E.*[2]

Boyarin argues that 'Judaism' as a religion is created over the centuries in dialogues with Christian theologians. I argue that such discursive production

---

[1] Daniel Boyarin. *Border Lines: The Partition of Judaeo-Christianity* (Philadelphia: University of Pennsylvania Press, 2004).
[2] Seth Schwartz. *Imperialism and Jewish Society: 200 B.C.E. to 640 C.E.* (Princeton: Princeton University Press, 2001).

is perhaps secondary to the machinations of state powers that had to deal with Jews as a conquered ethnic group within their jurisdictions. Schwartz' hypothesis that the village evolves as a 'religious community' within a state supports my argument that 'religions' arise as ways of granting attenuated powers to displaced governments.

Groups aspiring to have the status of 'religions' often use narratives that identify with former sovereignties both real and/or semi-fictional. Contemporary forms of Wicca, for example, posit an ancient history in which governments were organized according to the principles Wiccans now follow. Thus, Wiccans might be seen as imagining their covens as vestigial embodiments of previous sovereign governments. The nostalgic reference to a former deity or deities as a means of supporting current governmental power is a common theme in Western history and literature. I draw on my background as a classicist to highlight this trope in the *Theogony* of Hesiod in regard to how the reign of the Titans is cited when the Olympians triumph over them. I also mention Athena's treatment of the Furies in Aeschylus' *Oresteia*. In both cases, although the term 'religion' is somewhat of an anachronism in ancient Greece, the succession of sovereignties is nevertheless marked by relegating former ruling orders to the status of a cult, i.e, a vestigial state. Examples of the ritual citation of religious vocabulary as a way of authorizing so-called secular governments abound. President Eisenhower's move in 1954 to add the words "under God" to the US pledge of allegiance is one instance of how religion is conjured as a type of previous sovereignty on which present powers are based. Conceptualizing religions as vestigial states has value for clarifying matters pertaining to supposed qualitative differences between 'religious' and 'secular' law. According to my reasoning, such a distinction is more productively thought of as occurring between two forms of 'states' with markedly similar processes involving contingency, debate and compromise.

The hypothesis of religions as vestigial states can be of particular use for the analysis of gender in religion and politics. My interest in critical religion originates in my wish to restart the radical feminist work that used to be done in the subfield of "women and religion."

For years I had been attending academic meetings in which scholars who spoke about the topic saw themselves as representatives of their own traditions or as apologists for traditions that were the subjects of their research. Far-ranging critiques of sexist 'religious' beliefs, policies and practices, such as that of Mary Daly, had fallen out of favor. In its place was a quieter, more respectful spirit of reform. 'Religious' history was searched and mined for accounts of women who could be seen as clever agents within their traditions, as heroines who made the best of what was at hand, and as creative interpreters who found sustenance and inspiration in the seemingly oppressive texts and rites of their 'faiths.' Although the field of women and religion was flourishing in both divinity schools and secular universities, I was losing interest in an enterprise that I thought had abandoned the objective of political critique and embraced what I consider to be an attitude of advocacy for traditional thought and behavior.

I now think that feminist critical analysis in "women and religion" was blunted because the category of religion was not interrogated. While deconstruction of concepts and politics related to gender and sex continues to foster exciting theory with significant social impact, religion itself remains largely an under-theorized given. I believe that this tacit reification of 'religion' works both to undermine women's recent political achievements and to hinder further advancement.

Consider just these two examples: 1. From the U.S.: Citing the right to 'religious' freedom, former Republican candidate Rick Santorum proposed allowing states to ban women's access to contraception, a right won by means of court decisions in the late 1950's. Similarly, both Santorum and Mitt Romney, the front-runner for the 2012 presidential nomination, objected to the new US health care law's funding of legal abortions on the grounds that it could cause employers to compromise their religious beliefs. Several newly-enacted state laws now restrict women's access to abortion and reproductive services on religious grounds.[1]

In Afghanistan, the Karzai government endorsed a code of conduct asserting that women are subordinate to men, should not mix with men in work or education and must always have a male guardian when they travel. The statement thus suggests that the Afghan constitution that enshrines the equality of men and women is flawed from a religious perspective. Furthermore, violence against women as long as it is "sharia compliant" appears to be condoned.

---

[1] Efforts to restrict women's ability to access health care related to reproductive freedom are succeeding in the U.S. See for example, "Health Law's Contraceptive Rule Eased for Businesses With Religious Objections", *New York Times,* last accessed July 10, 2020. https://www.nytimes.com/2015/07/11/us/health-laws-contraceptive-rule-eased-for-businesses-with-religious-objections.html?referringSource=articleShare.

Such news supports the opinion of Fawzia Koofi, the Afghan politician and activist, who said that David Cameron and Barack Obama are supporting the Karzai government in talks with people who want to bribe the Taliban by limiting women's freedom using 'religious' justifications.

By proposing that religions be considered vestigial states at least in regard to law and public policy, I hope to suggest one way of countering arguments that restrictions on women's rights and freedoms for 'religious' purposes deserve more respect and attention than if such limits were to be put forward for merely 'political' reasons. Throughout most of history, governmental organizations have been based on masculine hegemony. According to the argument I am advancing, when governments are displaced they can persist within contemporary states as 'religions' that maintain their patriarchal origins and character. Since women's challenges to male domination have only met with some success in recent times within fairly contemporary forms of statecraft, if earlier states known as 'religions' are allowed too much authority over domains such as 'the family' or 'the home,' women will be the losers.

Works Cited

Boyarin, Daniel. *Border Lines: The Partition of Judaeo-Christianity*. Philadelphia: University of Pennsylvania Press, 2004.

Crawford, James. *The Creation of States In International Law*. Oxford: Oxford University Press, 2006.

Pear, Robert. "Health Law's Contraceptive Rule Eased for Businesses With Religious Objections". *New York Times.* Last accessed July 10, 2020. https://www.nytimes.com/2015/07/11/us/health-laws-contraceptive-rule-eased-for-businesses-with-religious-objections.html?referringSource=articleShare.

Schwartz, Seth. *Imperialism and Jewish Society: 200 B.C.E. to 640 C.E.* Princeton: Princeton University Press, 2001.

FEMINISM AND CRITIQUING CATEGORIES IN RELIGIOUS STUDIES

Cameron Montgomery

In the third year of my undergrad, I took a general method and theory course in the department of Religious Studies. We each had to write a research paper on an eminent scholar in Religion and Anthropology, Philosophy or Sociology. We went around the table saying who we would be studying. I picked James Frazer. A student in the class said 'Mary Douglas'.
"Who is that? That's not a real scholar," said the professor.
I was surprised because even as an undergrad, I knew who Mary Douglas was.
"Okay then, Mary Daly," said the student.
"No. Also not a real scholar," he said.
"Can I choose a woman?" she asked.
"You won't find one appropriate to study," he said.
He chose her scholar: Mircea Eliade.
Later I looked up more information on Mary Douglas: Princeton University, Oxford University, studied under E.E. Evans-Pritchard. She looked like a real scholar to me; what was his problem? Later on in the semester I mentioned Helen Keller in class.

"Who is that?" said the professor, and the whole class snickered with surprise. Embarrassed, he snapped at me.

"If she's some feminist hero of course I don't know her."

His words dripped with vitriol. I had no idea what he was on about. At that point I had never in my life heard the word "feminism". (Naomi Goldenberg remedied that gap in the fourth year of my undergrad.) I thought of Mary Douglas as a pretty stereotypical-of-her-time anthropologist of religion, and Helen Keller as an inspiration to anybody fighting against restrictive limitations, regardless of her gender.

It was not until I watched Owen 'Alik Shahadah and M. K. Asante Jr.'s documentary *500 Years Later* that I was able to put my undergraduate experience into context. The film explores the residual effects of slavery on contemporary American society. There is a scene where a white teacher stands in front of a classroom teaching about white history; the white kids are engaged and have their hands raised, and the black kids sit silent. The scene cuts to one where a black teacher adds content about non-white philosophers, inventors and great thinkers to the course, and the whole class is engaged. The voiceover explains that whitewashed education makes all these kids learn that there are no black great thinkers. When I watched this part of the film, I realized that my professor denying that women writers and thinkers even exist was actually worse than presenting and debating their ideas.

Little did I know during my method and theory course that Mary Daly's *Beyond God the Father* is one of the most important and brilliant texts in the field of Religious Studies. It is a classic that I quote on a regular basis and a necessary part of my academic repertoire.

As critical scholars lurking in departments of Religious Studies I think it is important to start with the basics, and state what by now to me is obvious, but is not obvious in the uncritical reaches of the field: Do you believe that women scholars are as intelligent, interesting, and important as the male ones? Then show it in your references and your syllabi. That is where the critical engagement should start.

My last major project was an ethnographic study of religion and women's activism in Ukraine and Turkey. Just because I was studying women, does not mean that my methodology was feminist. If I had accepted the conventionally reinscribed significance of the terms my participants were using, terms that this field uses without a gendered analysis, my approach would not have been specifically feminist.

For example, the term 'worship' gets used quite often in the field of Religious Studies. If your experience of worship is your brother reciting the kaddish at your father's funeral, while you, a woman, listen from behind a screen, then the foundation of your perspective on worship is different than that of your brother. In this example, worship can be defined as being heard, or alternately, as being hidden. The meaning of 'worship' is contingent on gender, but is a term that in traditionalist frameworks, like Ninian Smart's, for example, is defined as static, neutral, and 'obvious'.

'Faith' is another example of an essentialized term which is often used without a gendered analysis. I would argue that in most Christianities 'faith' for women means 'faith in patriarchal authority', while for men it means 'faith in self'. Simply studying women talking about faith, then, with 'faith' in your study defined as it pertains to men (or left undefined at default-maleness: see Simone de Beauvoir's *The Second Sex*), is failing to critically engage gender.

One of the basic binaries prevalent in the field is the religious/secular binary. (At my doctoral comprehensive examination, one of the examiners argued that this binary exists not only in the field but everywhere in the world, fundamentally. At my thesis defense, one of the examiners argued that it is not used in the field at all anymore. Which is worse? I'm not sure.) This religion-as-depoliticized-space vs. secular-as-politicized-space binary operates from the perspective of a privileged individual with access to mechanisms of self-determination, who is able to define 'religion' as a personal belief separate from a public sphere. For women, there can be no religion/secular binary because women's lives are always politicized.

Whatever women do with their bodies is considered a political statement. You shave your armpits? Political statement. You don't shave your armpits? Political statement. You wear something on your head? Political statement. You wear nothing on your head? Political statement. What you eat, where you stand, whether or not you are smiling, all of your health choices, everything to do with your sexuality—these things are political statements whether you intend them to be or not. What a man does with his body may be a personal choice, but women do not have that luxury. Adding 'religion' to the analysis does not change this basic fact of living as a woman. Women making choices about their bodies within the discursive space of 'religion' are not suddenly exempt from politicization.

In my ethnographic work with marginalized women, I saw time and time again that women making choices about 'religion' are considered activists and political agents. Women making any statements at all about religion are engaging in politics, even if those statements are identical to men's statements which are classified as 'personal' or 'faith-based'. Much work in a 'religion' space done by women is classified into the 'political' category and risks becoming 'non-data' in the field of Religious Studies.

Any study meant to include women which does not account for this in their methodological tools is missing an important dimension of analysis. Avoiding or neglecting to critically engage gender will only make research results lack relevance for potentially half of the subjects of study. Daly theorized that the "tyranny of methodolatry" keeps the perspectives of women unheard as "nondata" and translated through a male lens over and over until the methodology itself is critically interrogated:

> The tyranny of methodolatry hinders new discoveries. It prevents us from raising questions never asked before and from being illuminated by ideas that do not fit into pre-established boxes and forms. The worshippers of Method have an effective way of handling data that does not fit into the respectable categories of questions and answers. They simply classify it as nondata, thereby rendering it invisible.[1]

As Pamela Dickey Young points out, "method determines outcome."[2] At a 2014 'Expert Meeting on Religion, Gender, Sexuality and Activism' in Ghent, organized by the Religion and Gender Network, Sara Borrillo gave a talk on the methodological and ethical dimensions of doing feminist work in Religious Studies. She said that her work is not feminist if it is irrelevant to the women she studies. Discourses on religion are very often depoliticized. Depoliticizing 'religion' would make my work irrelevant to the women I study.

---

[1] Mary Daly. *Beyond God the Father: Toward a Philosophy of Women's Liberation.* (Boston: Beacon Press, 1973) 15.

[2] Pamela Dickey Young. *Feminist Theology/Christian Theology: In Search of Method.* (Minneapolis: Augsburg Fortress, 1990) 17.

Works Cited

Dickey Young, Pamela. *Feminist Theology/Christian Theology: In Search of Method.* Minneapolis: Augsburg Fortress, 1990.

de Beauvoir, Simone, translated by H. M. Parshley. *The Second Sex.* New York: Bantam Books, 1952.

Daly, Mary. *Beyond God the Father: Toward a Philosophy of Women's Liberation.* Boston: Beacon Press, 1973.

GENDER AND CAREER PROGRESSION IN THEOLOGY AND RELIGIOUS STUDIES

Katja Neumann

In 2013 Mathew Guest, Sonya Sharma and Robert Song published a report on Gender and Career Progression in Theology and Religious Studies published with SOCREL (the British Sociology Association Sociology of Religion Study Group). Detailing some comparative data in the field charted against the gendered profile of the discipline, the report highlighted a number of factors that influence women's pathways through academic study and career choices in academia that I feel are worth reiterating to our readers. While there are other Arts and Humanities-based subjects that are marked by the trends indicated in the report, in a comparison between English, Philosophy, Anthropology, Mathematics and Chemistry, the field indicated by Theology and Religious Studies (TRS) fared worst as regards a gradient decline of women enrolled in further study, or progressing through academic promotion procedures.

Whereas by and large female students outnumber male students in undergraduate courses, over the course of postgraduate work, taught and research, the figures begin to tip in balance. As the study shows, 'the drop off rate for female TRS students is more than twice that of any of these other subjects'.[1]

Of the numerous indicators gathered by the report, the 'gradual female withdrawal in tandem with academic progression',[2] a recurring theme was that of lacking confidence in women candidates. However, three issues stand out as especially connected to the academic subject area, rather than a patriarchal institutional culture underwriting academia at large: the recruitment strategies of some institutions that recruit from countries in which candidates are likely to be funded for their studies by their church, which may reinforce a conservative, gendered reception of Christianity also at a structural level.[3] To develop the level of confidence in female students to pursue a career path in particular sub-disciplines consequently appears as comparatively more problematic.

The report specifically names Systematic Theology amongst its finds.[4] A second area highlighted in relation to that of recruitment from elsewhere is the connection of TRS departments with denominational affiliation, often due to supplying training for ministry for which the recruitment by the churches into ministry impacts upon the question of diversity at the university.[5] And thirdly, the administrative struggle of TRS departments in their variously re-structured forms. Specifically, in the complicated relationship and disciplinary distinction drawn between religious studies in a broader, often interdisciplinary field, and theology, the report noted the implications on directions for research when targeting submissions for the REF (Research Excellence Framework).[6] All of these issues, in effect, are symptomatic of funding politics, as they come through at various stages for career progression: in recruitment, in funding further studies, and in impact assessment for career progression.

---

[1] M. Guest, S. Sharma, and R. Song. *Gender and Career Progression in Theology and Religious Studies* (Durham, UK: Durham University, 2013), 12.
[2] Guest, Sharma, and Song. *Gender and Career Progression*, 4.
[3] Ibid. 14.
[4] Ibid. 15.
[5] Ibid. 13.
[6] Ibid. 16.

Motivation to pursue further study, in my own case with the University of Stirling (one of the few non-denominational schools – and one without the competing demands of classical theology), had largely been kindled by a postgraduate initiative titled "Feminine Divine" that was run over the spring term in 2009 by research postgraduates of the interdisciplinary school for Languages, Literatures and Cultures to which Religious Studies at Stirling belonged at the time. As a first point of contact with the postgraduate community, the lively and welcoming circle of feminist postgraduates made a strong impression on me, as I shied away from approaching (our very approachable!) staff to discuss options of further study. In light of prejudices against tags such as "feminist," highlighted in the report,[7] I recall the reaction of one of my friend's parents, who upon hearing of their daughter's participation in the group, cautiously asked if her relationship to her male partner was still all it could be. The equation between the theme "Feminine Divine," feminism, and lesbian culture in the popular imagination gave rise to many a discussion since.

The question of funding, albeit related to other reasons and factors cited by the study, analysing the recruitment processes and circumstances of candidates, remained largely absent from their consideration – due perhaps to the focus and response of those interviewed for the report. Having been one of the 33.2% of female research postgraduate students in the figures from 2010-11 cited,[8] I vividly remember the apprehension in the run-up to deadlines for funding applications after the announcement of cuts in the Arts and Humanities, that could have very well spelled the end of my own academic aspirations. The prospect, particularly in a time of economic austerity, of finding part time work that could fund tuition fees and living costs, especially if there are no family savings to meet some of the costs, is not inviting. Looking back at my studies, I know all too well that without funding, I would have written a different piece of research, if at all: economic demands play crucially on the scope and outcomes of research, whichever the field.

Curiously, the report characterised Philosophy and English as two comparative reference groups for the field in light of working methods and subject matter within the Arts and Humanities, cited to aid the interpretation of the absolute figures attained from the Higher Education Information

---

[7] Ibid. 8, 16.
[8] Ibid. 9.

Database for Institutions (HEIDI).[9] I say curiously because in the logic of funders – and certainly in the historical development of Religious Studies – TRS nestles under the rubric of Historical and Theological Research.

While I do not have access to the numbers of female students progressing through a career in Historical Research, my estimate is that this line of inquiry might have found TRS less of a special case. Obviously this is not to say that it would therefore be any more acceptable to the health of the academic institutions to maintain this imbalance. Looking at the developments in the Church of England since the debates around women bishops in 2013, and ratifying the decision in 2014, offers hope that an institutionally symptomatic imbalance in the ratio of male and female students and academics (and as the case may be, clergy), that may have skewed the ratio of some institutions in the study in comparison to the national average,[10] is likely to change over the coming years by providing significant role models to an aspiring generation of women scholars.

Institutions and organisations are eager to pick up discussions to maintain a strong and healthy disciplinary diversity, and the annual 'Socrel Response Day' on the theme 'Achieving Gender Equality in the Academy: Intersections, Interrogations and Practices' (October 4, 2014) in London was an event of primary importance to raising awareness and facilitating discussions that prepare responsible leadership in academia for a future in TRS. Inspiring networking opportunities in pursuit of a robust mentoring scheme, central amongst the recommendations of the report, are encouraged in order to facilitate and prepare students and academic staff to face the challenges amidst austere times in pursuit of achieving gender equality in the academic engagement with TRS and beyond.

---

[9] Ibid. 10.
[10] Ibid. 13.

Works Cited

Guest, Mathew, Sonya Sharma, and Robert Song. *Gender and Career Progression in Theology and Religious Studies.* Durham, UK: Durham University, 2013.

CRITICAL RELIGION AND EDUCATION

THE MARKETIZATION OF THE ACADEMY FOR PROFIT – IS IT FOUNDED ON THE MYTH OF RELIGIOUS VIOLENCE?

Francis Stewart

"The Arts and Sciences, essential to the prosperity of the State and to the ornament of human life, have a primary claim to the encouragement of every lover of his country and mankind." –George Washington.

We are all too aware that there has been a growing sense of higher education as a marketplace, indeed a global marketplace, and that has brought some benefits. Increased access for researchers and students to wider and more diverse cultures, emerging academic schools of thought and discipline that rely upon globalisation, and some opportunities for the development of multi-cultural, multi-ethnic and multi-class interaction for a wider range of students. The benefits are based on the global aspect, so what about the marketplace aspects?

There we find a less positive picture unfortunately.

Multiple articles, newspaper columns and blog posts have been written about the over-saturation of administrative staff,[1] the cuts in funding[2] and the burden of time detailing and cost efficiency that results in increasing number of casual contracts for staff, especially young staff.[3] Often this is articulated as an attack on the humanities. While acknowledging that STEM subjects have received their own funding cuts, it is undeniable that the humanities have taken a stronger and more sustained attack for a greater period of time and is now, perhaps, reaching crisis point.

In the USA in 2011 humanities subjects received less than half of one percent of the amount of funding that STEM subjects received.[4] In the UK the situation is not quite that severe, but it is moving in a general downward trend. The implied meaning behind such an approach is that studying the humanities is not profitable because it cannot be sold on and therefore studying it at university level is some form of self-indulgence that should not be funded by the public purse. Accepting this relies upon accepting that higher education, indeed learning itself, has moved from a good (something for the value of the individual, community or society writ large) to a good (a commodity for sale) to use Charles Taylor briefly.[5]

There are multiple indices beyond funding that one can point to which also reveal this shift in global marketization of higher education into a profitable good.

During Thatcher's time (incidentally the only UK Prime Minister thus far who also served as Secretary of State for Education) there was the creation of the RAE (Research Assessment Evaluation) which later became the REF (Research Excellence Framework) used now to categorise, rank and centrally mandate the value of research. There are now endless performance

---

[1] P. Winston Fettner. "The Crisis in the Humanities and the Corporate Attack on the University," accessed 10.05.2019, https://www.academia.edu/875988/The_Crisis_in_the_Humanities_and_the_Corporate_Attack_on_the_University; Alex Preston, "The war against humanities at Britain's universities," *The Guardian*, 29.03.2015, https://www.theguardian.com/education/2015/mar/29/war-against-humanities-at-britains-universities.

[2] Ella Delany. "Humanities Studies Under Strain Around the Globe," *The New York Times*, 01.12.2013, https://www.nytimes.com/2013/12/02/us/humanities-studies-under-strain-around-the-globe.html?_r=0.

[3] Ferdinand von Prondzynski. "The casualisation of the academic profession," *A University Blog: Diary of life and strategy inside and outside of university*, 27.04.2010, https://universitydiary.wordpress.com/2010/04/27/the-casualisation-of-the-academic-profession/.

[4] Ella Delany. "Humanities Studies."

[5] Charles Taylor. *A Secular Age*, (Cambridge Ma: Belknapp Harvard, 2007).

reviews, peer reviews of teaching, student questionnaires and funding goals to be attained. These are all means of creating something marketable and profitable far in excess of student fees. Those departments which are seen to be less profitable or sellable, those subjects not so easily quantifiable in their outputs, are being pared down or closed down. Typically, these are the arts, social sciences and the humanities, especially in the UK.

So why is this and what does it have to do with critical religion? Obviously the first question has been partly answered above and in the links; it is for profit and global market forces. However, that is only part of it; the narrative of progress heralded since the Enlightenment that requires what William Cavanaugh refers to as a dichotomizing clash of civilisations that necessitates a myth of religious violence to be perpetuated ad infinitum. According to Cavanaugh this "serves a particular need for their consumers in the West… [And] constructs the former as an irrational and dangerous impulse that must give way in public to rational, secular, forms of power."[6]

In the 21st century those 'secular' forms of power are capitalism as understood by neo-liberal governments and shaped by the interests of huge multinational corporations. We should ask if the interests of those corporations and the forms of power they maintain benefit from creating binaries and categories in much the same way as 'religion' and secular' have been created and used in the West for half a millennia? It is not much of a stretch to argue that language used to make STEM more desirable over the humanities, social sciences and the arts is really the next step along the path that began with the myth of religious violence. In an apparently liberal, multi-cultural society it is deemed impolitic to use language which would suggest that those in power are devaluing or denigrating religious beliefs – unless, of course, they are seen as extremist and / or a threat to Western liberal democracy (read power).

Why is it then acceptable to do so for those subjects that study religion; a key part of everyday life, or those subjects that seek to understand how we create, organise, negotiate and recreate our world around us? Must everything be reduced to value added, and if it must why is developing an critical approach to thinking, developing a broader sense of what it is to be human not adding value to the lives of many students, staff and wider society? I would argue that it is adding precisely that value, but that value, that profit cannot be easily quantified, categorised and sold off and so is

---

[6] William Cavanaugh. *The Myth of Religious Violence*, (Oxford: Oxford University Press, 2009), 4.

negated. I would further argue that the sustained attack on the arts and humanities occurring throughout the West is a reuse of the language and categories such as to artificially separate 'religion' from the 'secular' and ensure the power remains firmly in the hands of those in one corner.

Stifling and closing down arts and humanities departments are not the march forward of the drive to progress, they are a repeat of the mistakes and prejudices of the past, they are a misuse of categorisation for the purpose of profit and a continuation of a false narrative about society: that it runs on dollars and pounds and not the ability, passions and skill of a myriad of different people. Collaboration and support should be the narrative, not division and destruction and if we fail to turn it around then we must, surely, stop calling places of higher and further education "seats of learning" and refer to them as what they have shown themselves to be – places of business.

"It is in Apple's DNA that technology alone is not enough—it's technology married with liberal arts, married with the humanities, that yields us the results that make our heart sing." –Steve Jobs, in introducing the iPad 2 in 2011.

Works Cited

Cavanaugh, William. *The Myth of Religious Violence*. Oxford: Oxford University Press, 2009.

Delany, Ella. "Humanities Studies Under Strain Around the Globe." *The New York Times*. 01.12.2013. https://www.nytimes.com/2013/12/02/us/humanities-studies-under-strain-around-the-globe.html?_r=0.

Fettner, P. Winston. "The Crisis in the Humanities and the Corporate Attack on the University." Accessed 10.05.2019. https://www.academia.edu/875988/The_Crisis_in_the_Humanities_and_the_Corporate_Attack_on_the_University.

Preston, Alex. "The war against humanities at Britain's universities." *The Guardian*. 29.03.2015, https://www.theguardian.com/education/2015/mar/29/war-against-humanities-at-britains-universities.

von Prondzynski, Ferdinand. "The casualisation of the academic profession." *A University Blog: Diary of life and strategy inside and outside of university*, 27.04.2010. https://universitydiary.wordpress.com/2010/04/27/the-casualisation-of-the-academic-profession/.

Taylor, Charles. *A Secular Age*. Cambridge: Belknapp Harvard, 2007.

CREATIVITY, ACADEMIA AND CRITICAL RELIGION[1]

Michael Marten

It is widely acknowledged amongst those who still care that academia in the UK is in very serious trouble. The most infamous embodiment of the current malaise is a quantification mechanism imposed upon universities by successive Westminster governments: a system of "research assessment" driven by an ideology of neo-liberal commodification. Until 2008 it was called the Research Assessment Exercise (www.rae.ac.uk); it now operates under the arguably even more Orwellian name of the Research Excellence Framework (REF, www.ref.ac.uk). Readers fortunate enough to be unfamiliar with the blight that is the REF may need an explanation: universities submit publications by their scholars to discipline-oriented panels, who then assess their relative "excellence" by awarding them numerical scores to indicate just how "excellent" they really are.

---

[1] Warm thanks to Jason Theaker (photographer and academic at Bradford University), who in a very helpful discussion alerted me to Mihaly Czikszentmihalyi's TED talk, and to the Critical Religion Association's Alison Jasper and Richard Roberts for helpful comments on a draft text.

Every department must produce an accompanying "environment" narrative that describes how wonderful it is – this is also numerically assessed. Finally, departments must submit so-called "impact" studies, which the panels assess using a series of specious measurements of the supposed impact of their scholars' academic work upon non-academics, an idea that barely works in the natural sciences, never mind the humanities. From all this, an overall score for the department will be given. That score, in turn, helps to determine the funding that the state gives each university. Of course, many academics and university bureaucrats have strong vested interests in these outcomes, indeed, the panels assessing individual scholars and their departments are largely made up of senior academics, clearly compromising their ability to engage critically with the structure.

The broader ramifications of the REF are apparent in numerous contexts, long before each REF submission deadline. Most universities end up appointing yet more managers, directors and deputy principals whose primary responsibility is to maximise their institution's overall score for the REF. It goes without saying that many of these people are on salaries that far exceed those of the academics they are supposed to be helping comply with the REF guidelines. Varying levels of competency, transparency and accountability characterise such institutional engagement, as conversations with almost any UK academic will verify. The REF and its implementation corrodes the UK academic environment on all levels (for example, in advance of the last REF, the ease with which citation records could be falsified in order to improve the supposed relevance of scholarly texts was demonstrated[2]). However, all this aside, one of the most important elements of academic thinking to suffer in this context is interdisciplinarity. The REF's structures do not cope well with scholars who cross traditional disciplinary boundaries, such as those working in Critical Religion. Even within the Critical Religion Association (CRA), it is clear that numerous disciplinary boundaries are being traversed by the scholars involved: literature, gender, law, postcolonial studies, art, history, politics, philosophy, music, anthropology, and a raft of other disciplinary descriptors feature prominently for each author.[3]

---

[2] "Gaming Google Scholar Citations, Made Simple and Easy," Phil Davis, *The Scholarly Kitchen*, last accessed January 08, 2019, https://scholarlykitchen.sspnet.org/2012/12/12/gaming-google-scholar-citations-made-simple-and-easy/.

[3] The author biographies of this volume are indicative of this variety; the list of scholars on the CRA website (www.criticalreligion.org) makes this point even more clearly.

Critical Religion is in substantial measure about questioning the boundaries and categories that are taken for granted in many contexts, and related to that, interrogating the power relations underpinning these categories – who benefits from such categorisations and whose position is strengthened by maintaining them? Whether this be about interrogating "politics", or "gender", or "interreligious issues" – there are innumerable categories that cannot simply be maintained in their present form without seriously distorting the very nature of human relationships. Whilst the CRA has its origins in the discipline of Religious Studies, even this cursory examination of the extent of the work being carried out under its auspices suggests that the Critical Religion Association should perhaps have been called the Critical Categories Association.

These disciplinary crossings form an integral part of the creative process. By its very nature, interdisciplinarity, because it is about traversing, even transgressing, traditional boundaries, involves a kind of creativity: how else can thinking beyond the confines established by a disciplinary tradition take place? Doing such thinking means that a certain kind of space must be available to the scholar, and although it will vary for each individual, no scholar I know can squeeze meaningful intellectual engagement with their research into half-an-hour between lectures. Creativity needs a different kind of space, a space that may well lead, for example, to a loss of a sense of time or awareness of one's immediate surroundings. In my own writing, I sometimes find myself working through the night on a chapter or an essay, not realising that I have completed eight or ten hours of intensive work – and outside it is becoming daylight again. These creative periods can lead to substantial leaps forward that push in some way at previous understandings, giving birth to new ideas or imagining new ways of interpreting old problems. I am firmly of the view that academic creativity is not substantially different to creativity in other contexts (though the forms it takes do, of course, differ).

Mihaly Czikszentmihalyi calls this experience 'flow' – the creative energy that enables us to engage our creativity to the full.[4] As Czikszentmihalyi explains, entering a state of creative ecstasy presupposes certain training and experience. In an academic context, the traditional degree pattern – undergraduate, taught postgraduate, and doctorate – is a way of gradually developing this experience within (as far as is possible)

---

[4] "Flow, the secret to happiness," Mihaly Csikszentmihalyi, *TED 2004*, last accessed January 08, 2019, https://www.ted.com/talks/mihaly_csikszentmihalyi_on_flow.

safe structures relevant to the stage a student has reached. Creativity, however, also needs more than just technical prowess, precisely because transgressing boundaries requires the ability to imagine something more, something beyond what has been imagined in the past. This is because the boundaries that we are seeking to overcome are frequently ossified and maintained (whether consciously or unconsciously) by vested interests, including senior academics whose reputations may be subverted and even upturned by younger scholars.

The REF directly hinders this creativity. It falls into the same category as the endless funding applications academics are expected to pursue (though given the ridiculously low success rates for most applications, they are often largely pointless, even whilst they take up huge amounts of time and effort) and all the other manifestations of commodifying academia,[5] though it is arguably more powerful than all of these others. Such manifestations can be seen as mechanisms that 'human resources management' (HRM) deploys in order to control the transgressive creativity of academic research. After all, although the REF ostensibly encourages the creativity that HRM desperately seeks to control, the REF's regimentation of research activity maps very precisely onto HRM's aims, not least through its reinforcing of traditional disciplinary boundaries. Hindering interdisciplinarity, requiring endless 'accountability' exercises be completed, and rewarding only certain kinds of work... all these management tools and more minimise the spaces needed for Czikszentmihalyi's 'flow' – or even kill such spaces off altogether.

And yet these hindrances should not be allowed to do that: as David Jasper (Emeritus Professor at Glasgow University) once remarked to me, in many years to come we may be remembered for writing an important book, but we will not be remembered for our funding applications – nor, for that matter, for our department achieving a certain REF score. As the REF continues to dominate academic practice and overpaid managers exercise ever more unwanted pressure on academics, I sincerely hope that mechanisms of solidarity, whether through trade unions or bodies such as the Council for the Defence of British Universities (www.cdbu.org.uk), can enable resistance to flourish in order to counter these attempts at the ever greater commodification of higher education.

---

[5] Ross McKibbin notes some of these in his blog posting 'In Defence of British Universities' (*London Review of Books*, last accessed January 08, 2019, https://www.lrb.co.uk/blog/2012/12/12/ross-mckibbin/in-defence-of-british-universities/. The LRB blog is an excellent source of similar well-informed critiques of UK higher education, collected here: https://www.lrb.co.uk/blog/tag/higher-education/).

Certainly, if we care about our universities and the scholars who work there, we must constantly reaffirm the principle that the preservation of creative 'flow' that leads to boundary transgressions is one of the things that really matters. In so doing, we may yet manage to subvert the rampant managerialism that is slowly but surely destroying UK universities.

Works Cited

Critical Religion Association. Last Accessed May 09, 2019. https://criticalreligion.org/.

Csikszentmihalyi, Mihaly. "Flow, the secret to happiness." *TED 2004*. Last Accessed January 08, 2019. https://www.ted.com/talks/mihaly_csikszentmihalyi_on_flow

Davis, Phil. "Gaming Google Scholar Citations, Made Simple and Easy." *The Scholarly Kitchen*, Last Accessed January 08, 2019. https://scholarlykitchen.sspnet.org/2012/12/12/gaming-google-scholar-citations-made-simple-and-easy/).

McKibbin, Ross. "In Defence of British Universities." *London Review of Books*. Last Accessed January 08, 2019. https://www.lrb.co.uk/blog/2012/12/12/ross-mckibbin/in-defence-of-british-universities/.

WHAT IS THE UNIVERSITY FOR?

Andrew W. Hass

The University is in a crisis. Even casual readers of the broadsheets know this. But the crisis is not what most people think, including those who run the University itself. The crisis is not that the University is underfunded, and therefore has to start cutting back on staff, programmes, and services. Nobody would deny the University is underfunded, and that the breadth and quality of education it once offered is now being seriously eroded. But funding is not where the real crisis lies. Cutbacks are just the symptom of a greater underlying problem. The real crisis is an identity crisis.

What, in this early millennium, and at this present stage of modernity, is the University *for*? What is its role in society? What is its fundamental *raison d'être*? We are being told one thing, and one thing only: it is to be an engine of the economy. It is to be, alongside several of other central engines, a crucial driver of economic activity. Government tells us this. Economists tell us this. Business tells us this. And now, increasingly, those who manage the universities – the Vice-Chancellors, the Principals, the top administrators – tell us this. And thus, as part of the economic machine, the University must become more efficient, more corporate, and run on business models that have proven effectiveness towards economic growth.

This all may seem sensible enough, especially as the global economy faces a post-pandemic recession in which every institution must become more fiscally aware, and more fiscally parsimonious. But the problem is that the University, as an institution, never began as an economic generator, run on the model of business. Nor have its main contributors, those who make the University what it is, the researchers and lecturers, ever seen themselves, except only very recently, and then not by choice but by coercion, as in the business of business. (The exception, we might think, are those in business schools. But I suspect even here its researchers and teachers see themselves as educating *for* business, not acting *as* a business itself.) Scholars did not undergo seven or more years of post-secondary education with the sole intention of fuelling the economy by providing qualified workers with immediately transferable research. Thus the crisis of identity. The University is being told it is one thing, but the very "cogs in the machine" do not, either by definition or by training, operate towards that end. They do not buy the metaphor of the machine or the engine itself. They do not buy the metaphor of buying. But they are now equally hard-pressed to tell us what they do accept.

The modern University has lost sight of its roots as liberal education. This is most salient in the area of the Humanities: the University no longer has a sense of the "liberal arts". Here, if we follow the theories of higher education that were forged during the 18th and 19th centuries in the West, "liberal" meant free from control of the State, from control of the Church, and from control of Business. This did not mean liberal arts subjects did not treat the domains of politics, religion and economics in their thinking. Far from it. But it did mean those ruling these domains did not set the agenda for research and teaching, did not dictate the curricula. Research was free to investigate all areas open-endedly, without being directed and governed by external agendas, or in today's world, by spread sheet logic and statistics. This was more than merely knowledge for knowledge sake; it was based on what it understood as the proper culturing, or cultivation, of humanity, and of the structures by which humanity should live.

Though, as Immanuel Kant says in his *Conflict of the Faculties*, the general populace "want to be led not by the scholars of the faculties (whose wisdom is too high for them), but by the businessmen of the faculties – clergymen, legal officials, and doctors" (Kant has in mind here the "higher" faculties of Theology, Law and Medicine, as passed down by the medieval university structure), truth cannot come to light until a faculty is given complete freedom to pursue knowledge outside of any vested interest.[1] For Kant, the faculty best positioned for such freedom is, we could easily surmise, Philosophy. As a "liberal" pursuit, research and teaching here, as for all liberal subjects, should be free to probe, to question, to critique, to innovate anew the very paradigms under which we might find ourselves trying to live our lives, or to better them. And these paradigms included those controlling the domains of the State, the Church, and Business (which are now "capitalised" in all senses of this term).

We presently have a ruling paradigm of liberal, free-market democracy – a politics so deeply entwined with an economic ideology (or a political ideology so deeply entwined with an economics) the two cannot be separated or distinguished – which, as a matter of course, is sold to us as truth. As this paradigm has now been so thoroughly imposed upon the University, we are left to wonder where the critical voices are who can, in the name of open-ended enquiry that, as Kant says, "admits of no command to hold something as true (no imperative 'Believe!', but only a free 'I believe)",[2] ask the critical question: Is this the best paradigm available? Is this the only one we should be cultivating, and at all levels?

It might be. I can't say I know the answer. But I do know the question needs to be asked, the matter debated, and no more than within the University itself. We need to address the fundamental issue of identity: what is the University now *for*? what is the University for *now*? And we need to debate this outside the context of a corporate understanding of balance sheets, of key performance indicators, and of government-led funding-driven research exercises. Must teaching and researching the disciplines of the Arts and Humanities necessarily lead towards some economic liquidity? Must careerism be the only motive for studying a subject like Religion, or Philosophy, or History, or Literature? No one is debating these questions within the academy.

And the crisis is precisely that we cannot, under the present paradigm, find the space or the time to debate these questions. We are too busy administrating our way through the system, too busy conforming our research projects to maximise our minimal chances of being awarded external research funding from sources wholly wedded to the ruling

---

[1] Immanuel Kant. *The Conflict of the Faculties*, trans. Mary J. Gregor (Lincoln: Nebraska University Press, 1979), 51.
[2] Kant. *The Conflict*, 29.

paradigm, too busy writing departmental narratives that align ourselves to economic justification, too busy adjusting to managerial restructuring, too busy trying to attract "customers" through marketing schemes, too busy trying to achieve top-rate status as teachers and researchers who validate the ruling assumptions, too busy simply trying to survive what has become a profession with its own deep psychoses.

My own area, the study of Religion (and Theology), like so many of its cognate disciplines, will never be able to justify its existence on the grounds of economic contribution, careerist employability or spread sheet empiricism alone. Nor should it have to try. But it does, like others, have a tremendous amount to add to the debate about ruling paradigms. As we know, it had a monopoly on this subject – for better or for worse – throughout most of the last millennium. And it should be given every chance to continue in that debate.

But the debate is not happening. Not in the halls of the government. Not in the aisles of the churches. Not in the boardrooms of the corporations. Not in the files of the so-called independent think-tanks. And not, worst of all, in the academic classrooms and research centres.

Perhaps blogs might be the only truly liberal sphere available these days.

Works Cited

Kant, Immanuel. *The Conflict of the Faculties*. Trans. Mary J. Gregor. Lincoln: Nebraska University Press, 1979.

CRITICAL RELIGION AND NON-WESTERN CONTEXTS

THE PERRY EXPEDITION (1853-1854) AND THE JAPANESE ENCOUNTER WITH 'RELIGION'

Mitsutoshi Horii

Under orders from American President Millard Fillmore (1800-1874), Commodore Matthew Calbraith Perry (1794-1858) commanded an expedition to Japan in the 1850s. After more than seven months at sea, Perry and his squadron finally reached Uraga, at the entrance to Edo (Tokyo) Bay in Japan, on the eighth of July 1853. The Perry Expedition carried a letter from the President of the United Sates to "the Emperor of Japan". The President of the United States, and Perry who were carrying this letter, meant by "the Emperor of Japan" in this letter was in fact the Shogun, whom the Japanese historically conceptualised as the Emperor's military commander.

The official report of the Perry expedition shows that the American conceptualised the Japanese ruling structure at that time with the co-existence of two Emperors: "the one secular, the other ecclesiastical".[1]

---

[1] Francis Lister Hawks. ed., *Commodore Perry and the Opening of Japan: Narrative of the Expedition of an American Squadron to the China Seas and Japan, 1852-1854: The Official Report of the Expedition to Japan* (Stroud: Nonsuch Publishing, 2005 [originally, Washington: Beverley Tucker, 1856]), 22.

The 'secular' emperor is "the Ziogoons [Shogun], or temporal sovereign".[2] The ecclesiastical, or 'religious', one is "the Mikado" (This is an archaic name for the Emperor of Japan), who "has not a particle of political power" and is "politically insignificant".[3]

This specific idea of 'religion' as separate from 'politics', through which the report conceptualises Japan's ruling structure, had been powerfully institutionalised by the American and French Revolutions and their respective proclamations of a new world order.[4] In this discourse, "'politics' refers to a domain of rational, problem-solving action separate from the irrationality of religious superstition".[5] From this perspective, when the Mikado was imagined as the embodiment of Shinto 'religion', as distinct from the ostensibly non-religious secular administration of the Shogun, it was the latter which appeared to be the rational domain of the ruling authority of Japan. Thus, the United States sent Perry to Edo (Tokyo) to negotiate with the Shogun, rather than Kyoto where the actual Emperor had lived.

Going back to the letter which was carried by Perry, it was drafted in 1851 by Daniel Webster (1782-1852), and was signed by President Fillmore. This was accompanied by another letter written by Perry himself. These letters contained the English words 'religious' and 'religion', though there were no equivalent concepts in Japanese at that time.

The letters were presented by Perry to the Japanese officials on the fourteenth of July 1853, at Kurihama (present-day Yokosuka). Chinese and Dutch translations were provided together with the English originals. However, it was the Chinese translation from which the widely-circulated Japanese translation was produced. This was the first time the Japanese had encountered the English language concept of 'religion'. The original English letters were translated into Chinese by the expedition's chief translator, Samuel Wells Williams (1812-1884), and his Chinese assistants. Initially, Williams hired his Chinese tutor named Sieh. This man, however tragically, did not make it to Japan.

---

[2] Hawks. ed., *Commodore Perry*, 23.
[3] Ibid. 25.
[4] Timothy Fitzgerald. *Religion and Politics in International Relations: The Modern Myth* (London: Bloomsbury Publishing, 2011).
[5] Fitzgerald. *Religion and Politics*, 7.

He died from opium addiction[6] in June 1953, a month before the important Kurihara meeting, while the fleet was still anchoring at Naha in Ryūkyū ("Lew Chew," as it was spelt at that time, or present-day Okinawa).

American officials acted quickly to obtain a replacement for Sieh from Shanghai in seventeen days. This new Chinese assistant, however, spoke Shanghainese, while "Williams could only speak Cantonese then".[7] Speaking different dialects, they had trouble understanding each other. When translating President Fillmore's letter into Chinese, Williams complained: "I have been busy translating the President's letter, and find my Chinese assistant a mere office copyist, one who has had but little reading and is not quick at catching my meaning".[8] He continues: "Added to this, his pronunciation differs from mine considerably, so that we are frequently thrown off from catching the meaning".[9]

In spite of these difficulties, Williams still managed to translate the letters which would be presented to Japanese officials at Kurihara. There is no doubt that Williams had expertise in Chinese language. However, with regard to the generic notion of "religion" in the letters, one can imagine that it must not have been an easy process to translate when the Chinese language did not have an equivalent concept, either.

Whilst translating President Fillmore's letter into Chinese, the phrase "religious or political" was interpreted as 政礼, meaning 'governance and rites'. By the mid-nineteenth century, the English language had already established the notion of 'religion' as distinct from 'politics'. In contrast, the Chinese terms of 'governance' (*ching*) and 'rites' (*li*) did not have the same binary relation as 'politics' and 'religion', and carry very different nuances. Whilst *ching* implies the ruling of a territorial country by the imperial authority, *li* denotes the code of human conduct encompassing both the private and the public realms. *Li* renders the general sense of propriety and etiquette, which cannot be confined in the modern western notion of 'religious'.

---

[6] Frederick Wells Williams. ed., *The Life and Letters of Samuel Wells Williams, LL.D., missionary, diplomatist, Sinologue* (New York: GP Putnam's sons, 1888), 28.

[7] De-min Tao. "Negotiating Language in the Opening of Japan: Luo Sen's Journal of Perry's 1854 Expedition." *Japan Review* 17, no. 1 (2005): 115, n. 26.

[8] Frederick Wells Williams. ed., *A Journal of the Perry Expedition to Japan (1853-1854)* (Yokohama: Kelly & Walsh, 1910), 44.

[9] Williams. *A Journal*, 44.

The Japanese version of the letter inherited the Chinese phrase 政礼 (governance and rites) in place of the English phrase "religion and politics". When it came to be bilaterally translated into Japanese, however, the meaning was once again transformed. In the mid-nineteenth century, the Chinese ideograph, *ching* 政, was read in Japan as *matsurigoto*, which is derived from the word *matsuri*, meaning 'to worship'. The concept of *matsurigoto* indicates that the purpose of human governance was "to celebrate the deities who created the realm and the people".[10] It contained an element which can be regarded as 'religious' in the modern sense.

As for the Chinese concept of *li* (rites), it was read as *rei* in Japan. While the Chinese concept of *li* represents the Confucian concept of propriety, in mid-nineteenth century Japan, the notion of *rei* was understood as norms of respecting existing social hierarchy. In this conceptualization, it is very hard to regard *rei* as the equivalent to the western notion of 'religious' as distinct from 'political'. The Protestant notion of private faith, as articulated by the term 'religious', was bilaterally translated into the Japanese concept of *rei*, as a set of cultural codes which encompassed the entire social practices, including governance.

A similar transformation of meaning can be found in the process of the bilateral translation of Perry's letter which accompanied President Fillmore's letter. Whereas Williams used the term *li* to translate the adjective 'religious' in Fillmore's letter, he chose the Chinese word *kiáu* 教, for the noun 'religion' in Perry's letter. As Williams' own publications in Sinology indicate, the mid-nineteen century Chinese notion of *kiáu* was much broader than the Western concept of religion as private faith. For example, the definition of *kiáu* in Williams's 1856 dictionary is: "To instruct, to teach, to show how; to command, to order; precept, principle, rule; doctrines, tenets; a religious sect, a school, or those who hold to the same opinions".[11] In addition, *kiáu* indicates a kind of hierarchical harmony between the old and the young, and between ruler and subjects.[12]

---

[10] Harry Harootunian. *Things Seen and Unseen: Discourse and Ideology in Tokugawa Nativism* (Chicago: Chicago University Press, 1988), 165.

[11] Samuel Wells Williams. *A Tonic Dictionary of the Chinese language in the Canton dialect.* (Canton: The Office of the Chinese Repository, 1856), 144.

[12] Samuel Wells Williams. *A Syllabic Dictionary of the Chinese Language* (Shanghai: American Presbyterian Mission Press, 1874), 372.

It is also a kind of teaching to be transmitted from the old to the young, and from ruler to subject.[13] The notion of *kiáu* was much broader than the Western category of religion, with a strong sense of ancestral traditions, which included families and the state. The Chinese character for *kiáu* was employed in the Japanese translation of Perry's letter. In the Japanese language, the same ideograph is read *kyō*. It is also pronounced *oshie*. As *kiáu* does in Chinese, the Japanese notion of *kyō* or *oshie* refers to the generalized idea of teaching or teachings. However, the Japanese concept of *kyō* or *oshie* seems to have moved away from the strong hierarchical connotation which is apparent in its Chinese meaning. For the Japanese, it meant a kind of systematic knowledge constituting the basis for public morality and the outward form of state ritual.[14] In this sense, it was likely that such things as the constitutional systems and state ceremonies in Europe and America, would have been categorized as *kyō* by the Japanese.[15] In this light, the tacit distinction between religion and the magistrate, which Perry made in his letter, almost completely disappeared in the Japanese version.

---

[13] Williams. *A Syllabic Dictionary*, 372.
[14] Jason Ānanda Josephson. *The Invention of Religion in Japan* (Chicago: University of Chicago Press, 2012), 161.
[15] Josephson. *The Invention*, 162.

Works Cited

Fitzgerald, Timothy. *Religion and Politics in International Relations: The Modern Myth*. London: Bloomsbury Publishing, 2011.

Harootunian, Harry. *Things Seen and Unseen: Discourse and Ideology in Tokugawa Nativism*. Chicago: Chicago University Press, 1988.

Hawks, Francis Lister, ed. *Commodore Perry and the Opening of Japan: Narrative of the Expedition of an American Squadron to the China Seas and Japan, 1852-1854: The Official Report of the Expedition to Japan*. Stroud: Nonsuch Publishing, 2005 [originally, Washington: Beverley Tucker, 1856].

Josephson, Jason Ānanda. *The Invention of Religion in Japan*. Chicago: University of Chicago Press, 2012.

Tao, De-min. "Negotiating Language in the Opening of Japan: Luo Sen's Journal of Perry's 1854 Expedition." *Japan Review* 17, no. 1 (2005): 91-119.

Williams, Frederick Wells, ed. *A Journal of the Perry Expedition to Japan (1853-1854)*. Yokohama: Kelly & Walsh, 1910.

Williams, Frederick Wells, ed. *The Life and Letters of Samuel Wells Williams, LL.D., missionary, diplomatist, Sinologue*. New York: GP Putnam's sons, 1888.

Williams, Samuel Wells. *A Syllabic Dictionary of the Chinese Language*. Shanghai: American Presbyterian Mission Press, 1874.

Williams, Samuel Wells. *A Tonic Dictionary of the Chinese language in the Canton dialect*. Canton: The Office of the Chinese Repository, 1856.

THE HARRIS TREATY (1858) AND THE JAPANESE ENCOUNTER WITH 'RELIGION'

Mitsutoshi Horii

Following on from the Perry Expedition, President Franklin Pierce (1804-1869) appointed Townsend Harris (1804-1878) in 1855, to be America's first consul to Japan. Harris opened the first US Consulate in Japan in 1856. He successfully negotiated the Treaty of Amity and Commerce (also known as 'Harris Treaty') of 1858, in which he inserted a clause on 'religion'.

Article Eight of Harris Treaty contains the clause on 'religion'. Whereas 'religious' and 'religion' previously brought by the Perry expedition, were understood either as the cultural code which embodies respect for the hierarchical social order (*rei*), or the generic category of systematic knowledge (*kyō*), translating the same terms in Harris Treaty involved the Chinese ideograph *shū* 宗, as the central concept.

The subject of 'religion' in Article Eight of Harris Treaty is stated in the three languages as showed in Table 1. There are five instances of 'religion' and 'religious' in the English version. Via the Dutch language, they were translated into Japanese as summarized in Table 2.

Table 1: Harris Treaty's Article Eight in Three Languages

| English version:
Americans in Japan shall be allowed the free exercise of their religion, and for this purpose shall have the right, to erect suitable places of worship. No injury shall be done to such buildings, nor any insult be offered to the religious worship of the Americans.
American citizens shall not injure any Japanese temple or mia, or offer any insult or injury to Japanese religious ceremonies, or to the objects of their worship.
The Americans and Japanese shall not do anything, that may be calculated to excite religious animosity. The government of Japan has already abolished the practice of trampling on religious emblems. |
|---|
| Dutch version:
Aan Amerikanen in Japan, zal de vrye uitoefening hunner godsdienst veroorloofd zyn, en des wege zullen zy het regt hebben, voegzame plaasten van aanbidding op te rigten. Zoodanige gebouwen zullen niet beschadigt, noch eenige beleeding der godsdienstoefening van de Amerikanen, worden aangedaan.
Amerikaansche burgers zullen gene Japansche temple of mia beschadigen of gene Japasche godsdienst plegtigheden, noch de voorwerpen hunner aanbidding, eenige beleediging of beschadiging aandoen.
De Japanners en Amerikanen zullen niets doen, dat berekend mogt zyn, godsdienstige verbittering op te wekken. De Japansche Regering heft de gewoonte van op godsdienstige zinnebeelden te trappen, reeds afgeschaft. |
| Japanese version:
日本に在る亞米利加人自ら其國の宗法を念し禮拜堂を居留塲の内に置も障りなし並に其建物を破壞し亞米利加人宗法を自ら念するを妨る事なし
亞米利加人日本人の堂宮を毀傷する事なく又決して日本神佛の禮拜を妨け神體佛像を毀る事あるへからす
雙方の人民互に宗旨に付ての爭論あるへからす日本長崎役所に於て踏繪の仕來は既に廢せり |

Source: Gaimushō Kirokukyoku, ed., *Teimei kakkoku jōyakku isan* (Tokyo: Naimushō, 1889), 754-755.

Table 2: Instances of "religion" and "religious" in Harris Treaty and their Dutch and Japanese translations.

English	Dutch	Japanese
religion	Godsdienst	宗法 shūhō (lit. sect law)
religious worship	Godsdienstoefening	宗法を自ら念する shūhō o mizukara nennsuru (lit. to devote themselves to their own sect law)
Japanese religious ceremonies, or to the objects of their worship	Japasche godsdienst plegtigheden, noch de voorwerpen hunner aanbidding	神佛の禮拜 shinbutsu no raihai (lit. showing respect and giving prayer to kami and buddhas); 神體佛像 shinbutsu butsuzo (lit. embodied kami and statues of Buddha)
religious animosity	godsdienstige verbittering	宗旨に付ての争論 shūshi ni tsukete no ronsō (lit. disputes over sect doctrine)
the practice of trampling on religious emblems	gewoonte van op godsdienstige zinnebeelden te trappen	日本長崎役所に於て踏絵の仕來 nihon nagasaki yakusho ni oite fumie no shikitari (lit. the convention of trampling on images in Nagasaki, Japan)

Importantly, the Dutch version contains the term "godsdienst," which was utilised by Harris Treaty as the Dutch translation of the English term 'religion'. By the early nineteenth century, the Dutch term 'godsdienst' had been defined in a Japanese Dutch dictionary as *kami ni tsukauru hito*,[16] which means 'those who serve *kami*'.

---

[16] Jason Ānanda Josephson. *The Invention of Religion in Japan* (Chicago: University of Chicago Press, 2012), 87.

The implicit notion of god in godsdienst had been translated as *kami*. This point is worth paying special attention to in the sense that in the process of bilateral translation, the English word 'religion' became associated with the Japanese notion of *kami*, which "means (etymologically) 'high', 'superior', or 'sacred'".[17] Thus, the English word 'religion' was likely interpreted by Japanese translators in the sense of the service to *kami*, which was also "usually accepted as an appellation for all beings which possess extraordinary quality, and which are awesome and worthy of reverence, including good as well as evil beings".[18]

Upon this semantic background of the Dutch concept in Japan, in Harris Treaty, the English language terms 'religion' and 'religious worship' were bilaterally translated into Japanese as *shūhō*, and as the exercise of *shūhō*, respectively. The Japanese term *shūhō* literally means 'sect law'. The concept of sect or *shū* also implies the idea of ancestor or the more generalized notion of tradition. *Shūhō* can be translated as "ancestral law" or "the dharma of the patriarch(s)".[19] It is also explained that *shūhō* "referred to the practice, regulations, and law governing each specific Buddhist sect".[20] In the Japanese translation, the two English phrases "exercise of their religion" and "religious worship" were both translated as "exercise of *shūhō*". From the Japanese perspective, what was given to Americans in this first part of Article Eight was the right to observe their Protestant sectarian practices as their ancestral tradition.

The second part of the Article assumes, in the English version, "Japanese religious ceremonies, or to the objects of their worship". This is a continuation from the general American preconception that the institutions such as temples and shrines were classified as 'religious' as opposed to the 'secular'.[21] For instance, soon after his arrival in Shimoda, Japan, Harris was being accommodated by the Japanese officials in a Buddhist temple, and he expressed his uneasiness about his residence.

According to his journal entry on the twenty-eighth of August 1856, he regarded a Buddhist temple as a 'religious' place in contrast to the purpose

---

[17] Joseph Mitsuo Kitagawa. *On understanding Japanese religion* (Princeton: Princeton University Press, 1987), 120.

[18] Kitagawa. *On understanding*, 120.

[19] David Liu. "The Ancestral, the Religiopolitical," in *Religion as a Category of Governance and Sovereignty*, eds. Trevor Stack, Naomi Goldenberg, Timothy Fitzgerald (Leiden: Brill, 2015), 145.

[20] Josephson. *The Invention*, 90.

[21] Mario Emilio Cosenza. ed., *The Complete Journal of Townsend Harris: First American Consul General and Minister to Japan* (New York: Japan Society, 1930), 213.

of his residence as 'secular'. In other words, the use of a Buddhist temple as the residence of a Consulate transgressed Harris' religious-secular binary classification system embedded in his conceptual map of the world. However, this kind of binary distinction did not exist in Japan. Harris seemed to subtly notice this. In his journal entry on the twenty-seventh of May 1857, Harris noted: "I must say that I never was in a country so abounding with priests, temples, mias, statues, etc., etc., where there was so great indifference on religious subjects as there is in Japan".[22]

In the Japanese version, the generic sense of 'religion' in this part of the article was translated into denotations of specific objects. For the Japanese translators, "Japanese religious ceremonies" meant various ritual activities related to *kami* and Buddhas. The Japanese phrase used is *shinbutsu no raihai*. The word *shinbutsu* literally means '*kami* and buddhas', and *raihai* "refers specifically to activities like bowing or making other reverential salutations or offerings".[23] Therefore, *shinbutsu no raihai* means showing respect and giving prayer to *kami* and Buddhas. In a similar way, the next phrase "the objects of their worship" was translated as *shinbutsu butsuzo*, which refers to embodied *kami* and statues of Buddha. Here again, in the absence of a generic term, Japanese translators directly named the specific objects that would appear in shrines and temples, which Harris would have self-evidently classified as objects of worship for Japanese 'religious' ceremonies.

In the third part of the article, the phrase "religious animosity" is rendered *shūshi ni tsukete no ronsō*, which means 'disputes over sect doctrine'. Here it appears that Japanese translators had to ponder what kind of animosity it is, and interpreted it as doctrinal disputes. The term *shūshi*, literally meaning 'sect doctrine' generally referred to "the doctrines and tenets of a particular Buddhist sect".[24] Importantly, combined to the first part of the article, the Japanese translators consciously or unconsciously introduced "a distinction that did not exist in the English original: the Japanese version guarantees *shūhō*, while discouraging *shūshi*".[25]

When the Japanese version was applied, it would have guaranteed American citizens the freedom to engage in Christian practices but deterred them from debating Christian doctrine. In other words, the Japanese version

---

[22] Cosenza. *The Complete Journal*, 366.
[23] Josephson. *The Invention*, 90.
[24] Josephson. *The Invention*, 90.
[25] Josephson. *The Invention*, 90.

grants Americans the freedom of practicing rituals but implicitly prohibits proselytizing.

Finally, the term "religious emblems" is rendered *fumie*, which in Japanese referred to both the convention of trampling on Christian images and these images themselves. The images used in this specific purpose had already been repeatedly referred to by Harris as "religious emblems" throughout the negotiation process. The adjective 'religious' in this context indicates the association with Christianity. However, the Japanese version adds to the end the phrase "in Nagasaki, Japan" (*nihon nagasaki yakusho ni oite*),[26] which is absent from the English and Dutch language versions. This Japanese addition has been interpreted: "This is clearly an attempt by the Japanese government to modulate the prohibition on *fumie* by ending the practice only in Nagasaki [...] rather than banning it throughout the country".[27]

I argue, however, that this statement is slightly inaccurate. It must be noted that in his journal entry on the sixth of December 1857, Harris noted: "This custom [*fumie*] has been confined to Nagasaki".[28] Importantly, Harris himself assumed that the practice of *fumie* was confined to Nagasaki. What the Japanese translator did was to highlight this understanding of Harris regarding the convention of fumie. The convention of *fumie* had historically been systematically institutionalised primarily in Nagasaki, and in some other places of the Kyūshū region.[29] In other areas of Japan, if the *fumie* ritual had ever been performed, it had been done in an *ad hoc* basis.[30] Given this, the insertion allowed the Japanese to continue *fumie* outside Nagasaki within the existing geographical confinement and mainly in an ad hoc manner.

In my view, the omission of "in Nagasaki" in the English and Dutch versions is equally important. It was likely provided those versions with two kinds of interrelated impressions which are absent from the Japanese version. Firstly, by not stating the geographical confinement of systematically institutionalized *fumie* exclusively with the Kūshū region, it creates a semantic vacuum which can be filled with an impression that the convention had been carried out throughout Japan. Secondly, it constructs a

---

[26] This phrase can be more accurately translated as "within the area administered by the Nagasaki magistrate office in Japan."
[27] Josephson. *The Invention*, 91.
[28] Cosenza. *The Complete Journal*, 466-467.
[29] Yakichi Kataoka. *Fumie* (Tokyo: Nihon hōsōkyōkai shuppan, 1969).
[30] Kataoka, *Fumie*.

triumphant tone of the narrative as if Harris managed to successfully transform the traditional custom which had been regarded as barbaric by the Christian civilization across the entire nation of Japan.

It discursively concealed the limited impact of the treaty upon Japanese domestic governance and the fact that the shogunate still managed to minimize American influence on its territory. It is not to say that Harris' effort was insignificant to mid-nineteenth century Japan. Harris' painstaking diplomacy, which resulted in the signing of the treaty, in fact triggered turmoil throughout the ruling structure of Japan and contributed to the shogunate's subsequent decline. Nevertheless, the omission of "in Nagasaki" had given a space of interpretation in which the scale of American success in Japan could be exaggerated. It functioned to echo America's self-image as the world's liberator, which told the story that the pagan barbarity of Japan represented by fumie, had now been triumphed over by the Christian civility of the United States.

While Harris repeatedly reassured the Japanese officials throughout the treaty negotiation that the American government had no intention of propagating Christianity in Japan, the English version does not express any sense of discouraging proselytizing activities. Harris did not highlight to his Western colleagues the fact that the Japanese were continuously negative against any Christian proselytizing activities in Japan. For example, when he summarized the result of his negotiations in his strictly confidential letter (dated twenty-fourth February 1858) to Sir John Bowring, Governor of Hong Kong, on the topic of 'religion', Harris triumphantly claimed that he had secured "Free exercise of religion, right to build churches, the practice of trampling on the cross abolished".[31]

More precisely, "free exercise of religion" and the "right to build churches" were granted for Americans within their treaty ports, and the practice of trampling on the cross was abolished in Nagasaki. Once again, the absence of geographical denotations exaggerated the scale of American success in Japan. The American media reported the signing of Harris Treaty as early as the sixteenth of November 1858, prior to the proclamation on the twenty-third of May 1859. The New York Herald of that date interestingly added a sentence which was absent from the actual treaty: "the Japanese also shall be granted religious freedom".[32] For many Americans, Harris Treaty

---

[31] David Hunter Miller. ed., *Treaties and Other International Acts of the United States of America, Volume 7* (Washington D.C.: Government Printing Office, 1942), 1058.
[32] Miller. *Treaties and Other v.7*, 1041.

might have appeared as if it had opened up an opportunity for Christian missionary pursuit across Japan.

Works Cited

Josephson, Jason Ānanda. *The Invention of Religion in Japan.* Chicago: University of Chicago Press, 2012.

Kitagawa, Mitsuo Kitagawa. *On Understanding Japanese Religion.* Princeton: Princeton University Press, 1987.

Gaimushō Kirokukyoku, ed. *Teimei kakkoku jōyakku isan.* Tokyo: Naimushō, 1889.

Miller, David Hunter. ed. *Treaties and Other International Acts of the United States of America, Volume Seven.* Washington D.C.: Government Printing Office, 1942.

Liu, David. "The Ancestral, the Religiopolitical." In *Religion as a Category of Governance and Sovereignty*, eds. Trevor Stack, Naomi Goldenberg, Timothy Fitzgerald, 143-181. Leiden: Brill, 2015.

Cosenza, Mario Emilio. ed. *The Complete Journal of Townsend Harris: First American Consul General and Minister to Japan.* New York: Japan Society, 1930.

Kataoka, Yakichi. *Fumie.* Tokyo: Nihon hōsōkyōkai shuppan, 1969.

THE "NO TRUE SCOTSMAN" FALLACY AND THE PROBLEM OF IDENTITY

Michael Marten

The philosopher Antony Flew (1923-2010) famously described a fallacy that has become known as the 'No true Scotsman' fallacy. It was even published in the (real!) *Scotsman* newspaper in Flew's obituary:

> Imagine Hamish McDonald, a Scotsman, sitting down with his Glasgow Morning Herald and seeing an article about how the "Brighton Sex Maniac Strikes Again". Hamish is shocked and declares that "No Scotsman would do such a thing". The next day he sits down to read his Glasgow Morning Herald again and this time finds an article about an Aberdeen man whose brutal actions make the Brighton sex maniac seem almost gentlemanly. This fact shows that Hamish was wrong in his opinion but is he going to admit this? Not likely. This time he says, "No true Scotsman would do such a thing".[1]

This analogy is often used uncritically in thinking about the way in which identity informs understandings of religion. For example, after the 11.9.2001

---

[1] "Obituary: Professor Anthony Flew," *The Scotsman*, last accessed January 08, 2019, https://www.scotsman.com/news/obituaries/obituary-professor-antony-flew-1-799918.

attacks on New York and Washington many argued that although the aircraft used to crash into the buildings were being flown by Muslims, "*True* Islam is a peaceful religion" and the perpetrators were therefore not true Muslims. After all, in this understanding, true Muslims would not kill thousands of people in an attack – and, of course, the vast majority of Muslims around the world condemned these attacks unequivocally. Maybe, therefore, even though they described themselves as Muslims and claimed the attacks were also religious in nature, the attackers were not *true* Muslims?

In a Christian context, we can see something similar happening. Most Christians of all main denominations and traditions would argue that, according to their Scriptures, killing others is prohibited. And yet there are plenty of instances in which Christians kill other people, often in vast numbers. We do not even need to look into distant history for that: George Bush and Tony Blair both professed themselves to be Christians, and yet they presided over devastating attacks on Afghanistan and Iraq that resulted in hundreds of thousands of people being killed. But if true Christians do not kill, perhaps neither Bush nor Blair are *true* Christians? Of course, such arguments could be made for pretty much any tradition.

This way of thinking, as Flew wanted to show, leads us nowhere. Can we really, in a meaningful way, comment on whether someone is a true Scotsman – or a true Muslim, true Christian etc.? It seems to me that the problem here is the reification of a position being taken by an individual that then becomes an identity marker. Hamish McDonald might have a certain idea of what a true Scotsman is, but this idea centres around an abstract imaginary of the concept of the "Scotsman" – and the Aberdeen sex offender clearly did not fit that image. Using that kind of fixed notion, we will never find agreement on what a true Muslim, Christian, or even Scotsman might do. We clearly need to find other tools.

Neil Smith and Cindi Katz, cited by Sara Ahmed, discuss the difference between *location* as a fixed point and *position* as a relative concept, and I would argue that this offers us a much more helpful way forward in thinking about the question of identities and positionality:

> In geographical terms, 'location' fixes a point in space, usually by reference to some abstract co-ordinate systems …

'Position,' by contrast, implies location vis-à-vis other locations and incorporates a sense of perspective on other places.[2]

If we understand self-descriptions of individuals in terms of positions, rather than fixed locations or identities, we might find it easier to comprehend the 11.9.2001 attackers or the Bush and Blair warriors. After all, a statement such as 'I am a Muslim', 'I am a Christian' or similar is usually made in relation to others: most obviously and most frequently affirming commonality or marking difference. It is, to use Smith and Katz, an implied location in relation to other locations, with a sense of perspective on other places. This kind of positioning changes all the time, relative to our context. We can perhaps understand this relative positioning better by thinking about Judith Butler's 'turning'[3] when a police officer calls out, 'hey you!' We change our position in response to the call: we turn to see if we are the one the police officer is addressing, and our position relative to everyone and everything else around us – not just the police officer – therefore changes as a result of that address, even if the call is not really meant for us. Our location might not have changed, but our position has.

This approach can help us in thinking through some of the language used to describe positions. We can understand the Muslim or Christian attackers and their statements of belief mentioned above as positions taken in relation to others, rather than as fixed locators or identities. This does away with the need to understand the true Scotsman problem in contexts such as those described above: we no longer need to find a way to explain that actually, *true* Muslims or Christians would never kill others – even if these *particular* Muslims or Christians did so. Rather, we can look at how these attackers *and others* who position themselves as Muslims or Christians (etc.) understand these contexts. Then it becomes possible to construct an understanding of the totality of these representations, intelligently assessed, and taking many different positionalities into account in order to inform a more complete understanding.

This also helps us to understand the adoption of certain kinds of language in contexts that at first may appear to be misplaced; in this sense it is very easy to see how some of the ideas underpinning Critical Religion could lend themselves to a simplistic racism and Orientalism. For example, it is

---

[2] Sara Ahmed. *Queer Phenomenology: Orientations, Objects, Others* (Durham/London: Duke University Press, 2006), 12.

[3] Judith Butler. *Excitable Speech: The Politics of the Performative* (Stanford: Stanford University Press, 1997).

important to think about how we understand an imam in Timbuktu who says that:

> Since the beginning of time Timbuktu has been secular. Timbuktu's scholars have always accepted the other monotheistic religions. After all, we all believe in the one God, each in our own way. ('Seit Anbeginn der Zeit war Timbuktu säkular. Die Gelehrten von Timbuktu haben die übrigen monotheistischen Religionen immer schon akzeptiert. Wir glauben schließlich alle an den einen Gott, jeder auf seine Weise.' – author's translation)[4]

A more doctrinaire (but therefore racist and Orientalist) Critical Religion scholar might protest: terms like 'secular' and 'religions' (perhaps as opposed to 'religion') are concepts that originate in a Western context, with little meaning in Islam, so why is this imam using them in this way? Does he not understand the genealogy of such terms? And yet: essentialising Islam in such a way, as if Islam in Timbuktu were the same as in Mecca, Beirut, Paris, Kuala Lumpur, Detroit, or London is a sign of a complete failure to understand the positionality of the imam. We need to take his statement seriously: he knows what he means with this language, and whilst we might understand the interview with the Western journalist as framing his comments, we also need to understand the Butlerian turn here: he is not (just, or even at all) necessarily moulding his language to suit her, the journalist, but is seeking to articulate a position that is clearly held and important to him – and in the articulation itself there is also a movement.

Seeking to pursue a constructivist position as far as we can possibly take it enables us to hear the imam and understand his reworking of the terms that we might have thought we already understood from our Western-oriented history of religion – we can clearly see that he is repositioning these terms and this language in adopting it and making it his own. Therefore, whilst it might be of historical interest that terms like 'secular' and 'religions' appear to originate in the West – and we can thank a number of scholars of Critical Religion, amongst others, for helping us more fully understand this branch of intellectual history in recent decades – understanding the imam's re-positioning and re-use of these terms more fully should enable us to begin to

---

[4] Bettina Rühl. "Mali: Krise ohne Ende," news story, *Deutschlandfunk*, last accessed January 08, 2019, https://www.deutschlandfunk.de/mali-krise-ohne-ende.724.de.html?dram:article_id=304205

better understand those who might appear to be the Other, leaving behind the No true Scotsman fallacy and our essentialist historical notions of what constitutes *true* belief, practice, or adherence.

Works Cited

Ahmed, Sara. *Queer Phenomenology: Orientations, Objects, Others.* Durham/London: Duke University Press, 2006.

Butler, Judith. *Excitable Speech: The Politics of the Performative.* Stanford: Stanford University Press, 1997.

Rühl, Bettina. "Mali: Krise ohne Ende." *Deutschlandfunk.* Last Accessed January 08, 2019. https://www.deutschlandfunk.de/mali-krise-ohne-ende.724.de.html?dram:article_id=304205.

n.a., "Obituary: Professor Anthony Flew", *The Scotsman.* Last Accessed January 08, 2019. https://www.scotsman.com/news/obituaries/obituary-professor-antony-flew-1-799918.

POSTCOLONIAL AND SUBALTERN RETHINKING OF CRITICAL RELIGION

Rajalakshmi Nadadur Kannan

The early 20th century formulations of Indian identity involved using the constructions of specific understandings of religion and gender. Critical Religion (CR) has provided a crucial methodology for understanding the workings of these ideological operators in identity formation within such colonial contexts. In this line, CR has rightly shown that constructions of religion/secular, sacred/profane dichotomies enabled the legitimisation of hegemonic colonial discourses. It is crucial for us to look at the question of 'how' these appropriations were carried out by the colonised.

Historical archives[1] show conflicting and complex narratives on the indigenous understandings and usage of religion both as an ideological category and as a term. For instance, the archives show that South Indian nationalists often used the terms religion, sacred, secular, science, and profane in their discourses on Hindu/Indian identity.

Much as these terms were appropriated, they were not necessarily used as the colonial narratives intended. Thus, whilst secular was criticised as

---

[1] "The Madras Music Academy Journal," *Music Academy*, accessed February 10, 2019, https://issuu.com/themusicacademy.

modern, modern here meant materialistic — that is pertaining to materiality such as corporeality (sex), objects (wealth), etc., and therefore, profane. Science was often seen as a 'Western value' that potentially contributed to materiality when it was not thoroughly grounded in spirituality as Hindu philosophy was. Sometimes, science was cast aside as 'not Indian'. This understanding shifted when science was used to define[2] Hinduism as superior to Western society. Science when grounded in Hindu philosophy was understood as a body of knowledge. Other times nationalists quoted medical knowledge from the ancient texts (for example, Ayurveda and the Vedas) to show that science was embedded in Hindu philosophy.

Thus, Indian nationalistic discourses used the language (terms and categories) of the colonisers to beat them at their own game, as it were. For CR, semantics are important for our understandings of these discourses, but nationalists' mere use of these terms should not be seen as their adoption of a colonial, Christian understanding of these categories. The nationalists indeed used these terms religion, secular, science, and materialism in some instances that pointed to a colonial understanding of these categories. However, there were other complex ways in which these terms were used. As we can see from the examples given above, these terms had multiple meanings depending on the contexts within which they were used. These also transformed depending on who the discourses were aimed at, whether the colonisers or the subaltern groups. For instance, the regional linguistic nationalism that was a subaltern counter-movement to the hegemonic Indian nationalist movements in South India often advocated the importance of rejection of religion, and embracing science as the objective method of understanding human nature.

Strongly grounded in Enlightenment values, these movements, whilst rejecting 'Hinduism' as a brahmanical religion, did not reject other faiths because their primarily objective was to hoist a counter-argument to what they saw as brahmanical hegemony. Arguably, the agenda of these movements swayed the way these ideological terms and categories were used.

This emphasizes the fact that we cannot assume that appropriation of the colonial categories was homogenous. We must delve deeper into these movements to provide a contextualized understanding of identity formations. Deconstructing ideological categories and doing away with them might clear

---

[2] Rajalakshmi Nadadur Kannan, "Performing 'religious' music: interrogating Karnatic Music within a postcolonial setting" (PhD diss., University of Stirling, 2013), 51-60.

the discourses of modernity clouding our understandings of historical, colonial developments. But it does not fully provide a postcolonial subaltern understanding of historical indigenous discourses. To put it simply, the question should not only be whether the term religion was used, and where they learned the term, it is to also ask how the term was used. To not take that into account is to make the mistake of succumbing to the orientalist discourse of a pre-Christian indigenous era when religion and secular were one and the same, and a Christian/colonial indigenous era where these distinctions were introduced, which the nationalists appropriated. This, then, would be a good example of Aditya Nigam[3] argues as a postcoloniality that is an echo of modernity.

If we look at the regional anti-colonial discourses, it is obvious that the indigenous nationalists had more agency than that. Subaltern Studies stands as a testimony to it. Perhaps, I should make a point very clear: I am not suggesting that we should abandon Critical Religion (and given the Critical Religion focus of this edited volume, that would be rather ironic!). But, if we are to provide a historical postcolonial subaltern understanding of religion, then we must move beyond (as in, add to) the scope of Critical Religion to listen when the said subaltern speaks. We now have two issues at hand: a) how do we understand the heterogeneity of anti-colonial, and nationalistic discourses; b) how do we listen when the subaltern engages with these heterogenous anti-colonial, and nationalist discourses?

In an article published in 2016,[4] I have attempted to answer the first question using Dipesh Chakrabarty's now famous theorisation of histories.[5]

Chakrabarty theorises History 1 as the 'universal history of capital' that abstracts labor as a function that is removed from its contexts, and Histor(ies) 2(s) as 'numerous other tendencies . . . intimately intertwined with History 1 . . . to arrest the thrust of capital's universal history and help it find a local ground'. At the outset, History 1 and Histor(ies) 2(s) can be seen as polar opposites; History 1 is the secular capital and Histor(ies) 2(s) are the indigenous traditions, i.e., religion. However, as Chakrabarty has

---

[3] Aditya Nigam. "End of Postcolonialism and the Challenge for 'Non-European' Thought," *Critical Encounters: a forum of critical thought from the global south,* May 19, 2013, https://criticalencounters.net/2013/05/19/end-of-postcolonialism-and-the-challenge-for-non-european-thought/.

[4] Rajalakshmi Nadadur Kannan. "Gendered violence and displacement of devadasis in the early twentieth-century south India", *Sikh Formations: Religion, Culture, Theory* 12, no. 2-3 (April 2017): 243-265.

[5] Dipesh Chakrabarty. *Provincializing Europe Postcolonial Thought and Historical Difference - New Edition* (Princeton: University Press, 2007), 47-70.

shown, Histor(ies) 2(s) are present in History 1 in order for the capital to function; rituals invoking the divine, such as worshipping tools for weaving, etc. Thus, within these indigenous contexts, religion/secular categories, with the emergence of capitalism, does not function dichotomously.

Rather the 'religious' is embedded in the secular to prevent a total takeover of the secular. However, this theorisation provides tools to understand only certain nationalistic discourses. For example, it points to the phenomenological aspects of orthopraxy. There is such a multitude of hegemonic nationalistic discourses that need to be acknowledged to understand how colonial categories were appropriated. Moreover, we must also look at how subaltern groups engaged with these hegemonic discourses – both of the nationalists and the colonisers. After all, it is rather evident that the methodological tools used to understand the hegemonic nationalist discourses cannot be used to understand the engagement between the hegemonic and subaltern groups.

Michael Marten's theorising of 'religious alterity' helps us to provide a better understanding of these discourses.[6] Discussing the missionary narratives in the Middle East in the early 20th century, Marten argues that the Protestant missionaries understood the native practices and faiths as an Otherness, an 'alterity', that was somehow 'religious' in a way. In other words, Protestant missionaries encountered practices and faiths that they saw as definitely 'religious', but understood them as an alterity, by Othering these native practices.

Christian missionaries in the colonies were by no means postcolonial or subaltern. Nor were their understandings of indigenous faiths and beliefs. But as Marten argues, it is important to understand moments of Othering 'whilst ... hearing and respecting the language used by the individuals being discussed'. How does this work pertain to the discourses of South Indian nationalists, and the subaltern groups? In using the colonial categories, South Indian nationalists were involved in two forms of Othering – a) towards the colonisers through consistent differentiation between their 'superior Hinduism', and the colonial 'Western values'; b) towards the subaltern groups that challenged their hegemony — here the distinction was drawn between their version of Hinduism and that of the 'degenerative' versions of the Others. Within these forms of alterity, the nationalists used 'religious' in multitudinous ways some of which are described above.

---

[6] Marten, Michael. "Missionary Interaction as Implicit Religion". Presented at Implicit Religion conference, Salisbury, 2016. The author kindly shared this with me.

I acknowledge the risk of arguing that the nationalist discourses involved Othering the colonisers. At a fundamental level, this would be akin to making a case for 'occidentalism'. That is certainly not what I am trying to do here. Rather, I am pointing to the indigenous nationalistic discourses that used similar, if not the same, language of alterity used by the colonisers (and the missionaries) to assert their position and agency in the domain of colonial politics. In doing so, they certainly indulged in 'religious alterity' with the subaltern groups. Acknowledging this would enable us listen to the language of the nationalists, and accept that they had more agency than what we admitted that they did. Acknowledging this would also provide us with a new methodology to listen to the ways in which subaltern groups responded to such alterity.[7]

---

[7] Marten. "Missionary Interaction as Implicit Religion", 2016.

Works Cited

Chakrabarty, Dipesh. *Provincializing Europe Postcolonial Thought and Historical Difference*. Princeton: University Press, 2005.

Music Academy. "The Madras Music Academy Journal." Accessed February 10, 2019. https://issuu.com/themusicacademy.

Yale University. "About Yale: Yale Facts." Accessed May 1, 2017. https://www.yale.edu/about-yale/yale-facts.

Nadadur Kannan, Rajalakshmi. "Gendered violence and displacement of devadasis in the early twentieth-century south India". *Sikh Formations: Religion, Culture, Theory* 12, no. 2-3 (April 2017): 243-265.

Nigam, Aditya. "End of Postcolonialism and the Challenge for 'Non-European' Thought." *Critical Encounters: a forum of critical thought from the global south*, May 19, 2013. https://criticalencounters.net/2013/05/19/end-of-postcolonialism-and-the-challenge-for-non-european-thought/.

WORDS DON'T COME EASY: AN EXAMPLE FROM JAINA STUDIES

Melanie Barbato

Jainism is increasingly included among the "world religions" with a growing number of books available for both academic and general readers. Typically, Jainism is introduced as an Indian religion with around 4 million members and with a strong focus on personal development through non-violence and asceticism. The BBC website, for example, states that "Jainism is an ancient religion from India that teaches that the way to liberation and bliss is to live lives of harmlessness and renunciation."[1]

However, when I spoke to Jainas as part of my doctoral research in Karnataka, I found that many Jainas object to the idea that Jainism is their religion. For example, a lecturer at a Jainology department told me that he considered there to be only one true religion, and that would not be Jainism but non-violence. A bhattaraka, a highly venerated Digambara functionary, said that every religion claims to have the ultimate solution, but when new problems arise, subgroups will just form new religions, and that to him race, caste or religion did not matter for defining a person.

---

[1] "Jainism at a glance," *BBC*, last modified 27.08.2009, http://www.bbc.co.uk/religion/religions/jainism/ataglance/glance.shtml.

Another bhattaraka told me that Jaina dharma, Christ dharma and Muslim dharma were all limited but that the universe was unlimited. All these people shared an aversion against having their Jaina beliefs and practices categorised as religion not because they believed in the superiority of secular labels but because to them fencing off a part of reality as "religion" or "Jainism" carried connotations of a narrow-minded ideology and arbitrary boundaries. This highlighted a problem I experienced again and again when trying to write about Jaina teachings: what concepts and phrases do I use for talking about what Jainas believe and do?

My doctoral research focused on anekantavada, the Jaina teaching that every object in the world has infinitely many aspects even though only a limited amount of information can at any single point in time be grasped by human perception or expressed by human language. In that respect anekantavada is a philosophical teaching that involves questions of ontology and epistemology. But anekantavada is also one of the most important teachings of Indian rhetoric or, as the study of argumentation in India is commonly called, Indian logic. If objects have infinitely many aspects, this impacts the way we should speak about reality, especially in arguments about ultimate meaning. The claim is that ideally the expression "from a certain perspective" should be added to every statement, to show that it reflects only one of many equally justified possibilities. This has strong ethical implications which have become predominant in contemporary discussions about anekantavada as "tolerance". However, anekantavada also has to be seen in the light of the ultimate goal of the Jaina, becoming an omniscient, a liberated being who can grasp at will all aspects of past, present and future simultaneously. According to Jainism these omniscients, who have cleansed their souls through right conduct and knowledge of karmic particles, already exist in higher spheres. Anekantavada tries to show the limitations of human perception while bringing us as closely as possible to the reality of the omiscients. So is anekantavada a religious teaching?

I found that anekantavada cannot be properly understood if it is labelled either philosophy or religion, so throughout my dissertation I kept somewhat unhappily repeating the expression "Jaina philosophy and religion". Trying to avoid controversial terminology I also spoke of the "Jaina worldview" though I was not happy at all with this term because it lacked the emphasis on praxis.

Just using Indian terms did not seem a solution to me either because an important part of my dissertation was explaining an element of one culture for the readership of another. Of course concepts overlap and there are ways of explaining how they are connected but every concrete text passage calls for a concrete choice. It does, after all, make a big difference if I write that anekantavada is part of "Indian logic" or "Jaina rhetoric".

I cannot say that I have found a solution to this problem of categories and terminology but I try to make the tensions visible in the text. A first point was to reflect the different conceptualisations in the structure of my text. Anekantavada is about the many perspectives one can have on the world, and I therefore discuss in one chapter anekantavada as part of ontology, in another as part of epistemology, in another as soteriology. Then I try to bring them together in an overarching, more organic section, hoping that every time I present anekantavada in one way the other presentations will have some presence in the reader's mind. The other point was that I decided to provide a substantial amount of background information on terms that should not appear natural but contested. When I speak of anekantavada as being part of Indian logic I devote a whole section to discussing the field of Indian logic in comparison to Western logic, and that it is based on rhetoric and grammar, not mathematics. I thereby hope to draw mental landscapes that present a realistic impression even if the embedded terminology remains deficient.

I am not sure if the Jainas I spoke to in India would agree with how I present their tradition in my thesis and subsequent book Jain Approaches to Plurality, but I hope they would acknowledge that at least I have learned a lesson from anekantavada about the complexity of the world and the limitations of language.

Works Cited

Barbato, Melanie. *Jain Approaches to Plurality: Identity as Dialogue*. Leiden: Brill, 2017.

BBC, "Jainism at a glance." Last modified 27.08.2009. http://www.bbc.co.uk/religion/religions/jainism/ataglance/glance.shtml.

WHO DEFINES RELIGION IN THE COLONY?

Alexander Henley

On 1 September 1920, French General Henri Gouraud proclaimed the new state of Lebanon, or *Grand Liban*, from the steps of the colonial High Commission in Beirut. He did so as he took care to remind his audience, 'In the presence of the Lebanese authorities, the sons of the most illustrious families, [and] the spiritual heads of all confessions and all rites'. Photographs of the event show Gouraud flanked by these 'spiritual heads', with places of honour given to the Maronite (Christian) patriarch on his right, and the Sunni (Muslim) mufti on his left. The Frenchman used this highly symbolic foundational moment to consecrate the notion of Lebanon as a consensus between its Christian and Muslim communities, represented by patriarch and mufti.

The extraordinary paradox here is that this confessional representation performed two apparently contradictory symbolic feats. It intentionally and overtly lent the authority of these two religious leaders to the legitimation of the state. Yet at the same time it subtly and perhaps unwittingly (re)created the religious leaderships that these two gentlemen were seen to embody, precisely by presuming them to hold the authority to represent 'the Christians' and 'the Muslims'.

Ilyas Huwayyik, the man styled by the Maronite Church as Patriarch of Antioch and All the East, was addressed by General Gouraud as 'the Grand Patriarch of Lebanon'. Notwithstanding the dozen or more non-Maronite Churches that now found themselves within Lebanon's borders, many of which had protested the new state, Huwayyik and his successors ever since have been treated in state protocol and public discourse as spiritual head of all Lebanon's Christians. On Gouraud's other side was Mustafa Naja, the Mufti of Beirut, a judicial functionary appointed by the Ottoman Sultan to produce fatwas, written legal opinions. The son of a Beiruti perfume-seller, Naja's daily routine involved issuing fatwas to the public from a market-stall near the central mosque; holding a regular study circle in the mosque and participating in Sufi gatherings; championing an Islamic educational charity; and helping at his father's stall in the souq.

Naja resisted General Gouraud's designs on him. Proudly loyal to Arab nationalism, the mufti had initially refused to attend the celebration of a Lebanese state. The general is said to have threatened him with deportation. On the steps of the French High Commission, the reluctant Naja was symbolically cast as the Patriarch of Lebanon's opposite number, implicitly now the Mufti of Lebanon, religious leader of the country's Muslims. The French offered Naja the official title of 'Mufti of the State of Greater Lebanon', but he rejected it right up to his death in 1932. Nevertheless, he had been set on the national stage and a continued public role came to be expected of him not only by the colonial authorities but also by Lebanese Muslims seeking representation. Gouraud had orchestrated an iconic image of a national Grand Muftiship, and in the decades after 1920 that image would become an institutional reality. Naja's successor, Muhammad Tawfiq Khalid, took the title 'Mufti of the Lebanese Republic' and built up a national religious administration with an impressive Beirut headquarters that became the hub of a newly self-identifying confessional community.

This story seems in many ways a striking example of the transformative power of the colonial language of religion. John Zavos has shown representation as the means by which religion or religions were objectified in India, with the colonisers' creation of new public spaces as a key part of that process.

In Lebanon, as in India, 'representation translated into power through the articulation of firm, clearly recognizable communities'.[1] A French colonial official's selection of Mufti Naja to represent one of Lebanon's religions, as equal and equivalent to the representatives of other religions, empowered the mufti and articulated a new Muslim identity as a religious community. The mufti would not previously have been called a 'religious leader'. Indeed his office would not have been described as 'religious' in the modern sense: his role was judicial, salaried from a public budget and serving society at large. Similarly, Sunni Muslims in Ottoman society were simply ordinary citizens; they did not organise or conceive of themselves as a community in contradistinction to others.

The translation of the modern Western concepts of religion and religious into the Arabic words dīn and dīnī was accompanied by an exponential increase in their use, and an even more marked rise of the plural adyān. Only in the modern era was Middle Eastern society said to comprise a number of adyān; ministries were dedicated to 'religious affairs' (al-shu'ūn al-dīnīyya), staffed by professional 'men of religion' (rijāl al-dīn). In Lebanon the Mufti of Beirut was gradually elevated to leader of this religious corps (ra'īs al-silk al-dīnī), and finally to religious leader of the community (ra'īs al-tā'ifa al-dīnī). But just because change happened during this period, should we assume it was all driven by colonialism? The usage of dīn has no doubt changed, but were there not similar concepts in pre-modern Islamic societies? 'You have your dīn and I have my dīn', says the Qur'an. Classical thought opposes dīn and dunyā, the material world. The Ottoman notion of milla recognised the rights of non-Muslim communities. And the role of muftis – while judicial – was not merely legal in the modern sense: it was to define the proper practice of Islam.

The critical religion school has taught us to see the colonial invention of world religions and their relegation to a private sphere demarcated by modern states. But an emphasis on the bulldozing force of colonial power may obscure the resilience of local histories.

Mufti Naja may have been an unwilling participant in the colonial enterprise, but the rise of state muftis across the Middle East suggests that he was somehow an obvious, not an arbitrary, choice for the new role of religious leadership. Whoever defined religion in the new Lebanon, its result

---

[1] John Zavos. "Representing religion in colonial India," in *Rethinking Religion in India: The colonial construction of Hinduism*, eds. Esther Bloch, Marianne Keppens, and Rajaram Hegde (London: Routledge, 2010), 66.

was not simply marginalisation from a secular public sphere but by contrast the empowerment of new religious institutions and a lasting ambiguity over the nature, boundaries and even the possibility of 'secular' politics.

Works Cited

Zavos, John. "'Representing religion in colonial India." In *Rethinking Religion in India: The colonial construction of Hinduism*. Edited by Esther Bloch, Marianne Keppens, and Rajaram Hegde, 56-68. London: Routledge, 2010.

SOME (MAINLY) VERY APPRECIATIVE COMMENTS ON BRENT NONGBRI'S *BEFORE RELIGION: A HISTORY OF A MODERN CONCEPT*

Naomi Goldenberg

In *Before Religion: A History of a Modern Concept* (New Haven and London: Yale, 2013), Brent Nongbri makes a significant contribution to Critical Religion that will be useful to both students and theorists.[1] This is a clear and carefully written book, well researched and informatively referenced. Nongbri's strength lies in his feeling for antiquity. With precision and skill, he reviews English translations of the word religion in influential early Greek, Roman and Arabic texts to argue that the term is an anachronism supporting the conventional notion that 'religion' refers to a recognizable and timeless phenomenon. Although such insight will be familiar to readers of the works of Timothy Fitzgerald, David Chidester, Richard King, Russell McCutcheon et al., Nongbri's account is particularly notable for its sustained clarity and judicious selection of ancient source material.

Nongbri tells us that his questioning of the universality of "religion" began when he realized that the word did not exist in the Khasi language his

---

[1] Brent Nongbri. *Before Religion: A History of a Modern Concept* (New Haven and London: Yale University Press, 2013).

father grew up speaking in northeastern India. Instead of referring to specific "religious" ideas or behavior that could be distinguished from "secular" varieties, "ka niam", the Khasi term his father offered as an equivalent to religion, simply means "customs" in a broad sense. Further inquiry revealed that niam is actually a Bengali term signifying "rules" or "duties." This discovery about his paternal tongue forms the paradigm that Nongbri identifies again and again in his investigation of ancient sources. As he leads his readers through myriad texts of early history, he points to the absence of "the modern concept of religion" and how the insertion of the word misrepresents authorial intentions.

Nongbri structures his arguments memorably around a few well-articulated themes. His chapter titled "Some (Premature) Births of Religion in Antiquity" is especially effective. Under this heading, he refutes claims that "religion" emerged in reference to the Maccabean revolt, in Cicero's rhetoric, in Eusebius' texts, or in Muhammed's innovations. He also does an impressive job of showing that the tenets Tomoko Masuzawa identifies in the nineteenth century as formative for a discourse of world religions are actually well underway in the seventeenth century in the work of Alexander Ross *et al*.

Nongbri is convinced that the study of antiquity could be improved if "students of the ancient world [were] ... to work on generating a better vocabulary for talking about the various ways that ancient peoples conceptually carved out their worlds, a better means of describing the clusters of practices and beliefs outlined by ancient authors...".[2] He writes that the task is not one of finding a better word for "it" – i.e. of uncovering what "religion" meant in antiquity – but rather of realizing that there never was an "it" in the first place. Nongbri believes that if his advice were heeded, we would not wind up with more "slightly tweaked" books about early religions, but rather with more specific and insightful studies on such subjects as "Athenian appeals to ancestral tradition, Roman ethnicity, Mesopotamian scribal praxis, Christian and Muslim heresiological discourses, and other topics that will encapsulate and thoroughly rearrange those bits and pieces of what we once gathered together as 'ancient religions'".[3]

I suggest that Nongbri's counsel for reforming the study of ancient history should be applied throughout the field of Religious Studies. Nongbri

---

[2] Brent Nongbri. *Before Religion*, 53.
[3] Ibid. 159.

hesitates to recommend such an approach to scholars of contemporary "religions." Instead, he concludes his book with what I find to be a contradictory and confusing call to "think outside of our usual categories"[4] by being aware that whenever we use the word 'religion' we are employing a "second-order" redescriptive concept. Surprisingly, Nongbri says that such a conscious – yet, to my mind, impossibly acrobatic – use of the term could even have some benefits in the study of antiquity. Thus, in his conclusion, he momentarily argues against the thrust of his own conscientious analysis.

Despite this brief retreat from the implications of his critique, Nongbri succeeds in building a solid case for historians of antiquity to purge their intellectual toolbox of a distorting anachronism. In addition, his book also points to similar confusions and misrepresentations that occur with the use of 'religion' in reference contemporary times when the word is imposed on non-Western cultures like his father's or when scholars continue to use rhetorical ploys such as "embedded religion" to reinscribe religion as "eternally present".[5]

The argument that Nongbri frames so clearly and competently in relation to ancient history is applicable in present times and possibly more urgent. By assuming that religion is an eternal and universal "it" that identifies a bounded sphere of human life, distinct from what we term "politics" or "economics" or "the secular," we are doing more than hampering our understanding of epochs in the past. We are also obscuring our ability to see through the veils of ideologies that currently surround us. The task of lifting these veils, or, at least, of making them less opaque is one way to conceive of an objective for "Critical Religion" – an aim that Nongbri's work helps to further.

---

[4] Ibid. 159.
[5] Ibid. 152.

Works Cited

Nongbri, Brent. *Before Religion: A History of a Modern Concept*. New Haven and London: Yale University Press, 2013.

AUTHOR BIOGRAPHIES

Melanie Barbato holds a doctorate in Indology and Religious Studies from LMU Munich. She is the author of *Jain Approaches to Plurality: Identity as Dialogue* (Leiden: Brill, 2017), and has co-edited a book on the media and the modern papacy. Her current research studies what different high-level actors do when they talk about doing interreligious dialogue. Her project at WWU Münster examines the role of the Vatican and the World Council of Churches in Hindu-Christian relations.

Fiona Darroch is Book Reviews Editor for *Literature and Theology: An International Journal of Religion, Theory and Culture* (Oxford: Oxford University Press). She is a member of teaching staff in Religion at the University of Stirling, Scotland. Her research focuses on postcolonial literature (predominantly Caribbean literature) and representations of 'religion', particularly the politics of the term 'religion'. Her publications include:
Memory and Myth: Postcolonial Religion in Contemporary Guyanese Fiction and Poetry (Amsterdam: Rodopi, 2009), "Re-imagining the Sacred in Caribbean Literature" in Walton, Heather (ed), *Literature and Theology: New Interdisciplinary Spaces* (London: Ashgate, 2011).

Timothy Fitzgerald is one of the founder members of the Critical Religion Association. He was Reader in Religion at the University of Stirling from 2001 to 2015. Before coming to Scotland, he lived in Japan for 13 years (1988-2001). Among his publications on Critical Religion are the monographs *The Ideology of Religious Studies* (Oxford: OUP, 2000), *Discourse on Civility and Barbarity: a critical history of religion and related categories* (Oxford: OUP, 2007) and *Religion and Politics in International Relations* (London: Bloomsbury, 2011) as well as two edited books: T. Fitzgerald (ed.), *Religion and the Secular in Colonial Contexts* (Sheffield: Equinox, 2007); and T. Stack, N. Goldenberg and T. Fitzgerald (eds.) *Religion as a Category of Governance and Sovereignty* (Leiden: Brill, 2014). He has also published in the on-line journal *Critical Research on Religion*:
"Critical Religion and Critical Research on Religion: A response to the April 2016 Editorial", Critical Research on Religion, vol. 4, 3: pp. 307-313 (2016).

"Critical Religion and Critical Research on Religion: Religion and Politics as Modern Fictions", *Critical Research on Religion*, vol. 3, 3: pp. 303-319 (2015).

A full list of his publications can be found at http://criticaltheoryofreligion.org/timothy-fitzgerald/

Naomi Goldenberg, PhD (1976), Yale University, is Professor of Religious Studies in the Department of Classics and Religious Studies and former Director of Women's Studies at the University of Ottawa in Canada. Her publications include: *Resurrecting the Body: Feminism, Religion and Psychoanalysis* (Spring Valley: Crossroad, 1993) and *Changing of the Gods: Feminism and the End of Traditional Religions* (Boston: Beacon, 1979). She has co-edited *Religion as a Category of Governance and Sovereignty* (Leiden: Brill, 2015) with Trevor Stack and Timothy Fitzgerald, and is completing *The End of Religion: Feminist Reappraisals of the State* (Abingdon: Routledge, forthcoming 2021) with Kathleen McPhillips. Her book *The Religious is Political: An Argument for Understanding Religions as Vestigial States* is in progress.

Andrew W. Hass is Reader in Religion at the University of Stirling. His interests and publications operate at the intersection of religion, philosophy, theology, critical theory, hermeneutics, literature, and art, with particular interest in the idea of nothing [*Auden's O: The Loss of One's Sovereignty in the Making of Nothing* (New York: SUNY Press, 2013)], of negation [*Hegel and the Art of Negation* (London: IB Tauris, 2014)], and more recently, of silence [*The Music of Theology: Language-Space-Silence*, with M. Martinson and L. Ten Kate (Abingdon: Routledge, forthcoming). He is General Secretary of The International Society for Religion, Literature and Culture, and was general editor of the *Literature and Theology: An International Journal of Religion, Theory and Culture*.

Alexander Henley is a Marie Curie Fellow in the Faculty of Theology and Religion at the University of Oxford. He is an anthropological historian interested in how new conceptions of 'religion' have transformed the institutional structures of Islam in the modern Middle East. He has founded a research network on 'Categories of Religion and the Secular in Islam' to encourage and support an emerging sub-field at the intersection of Critical Religion and Islamic Studies. Alexander has held fellowships at Harvard and Georgetown Universities, and studied at the Universities of Manchester, Edinburgh, Durham and Damascus.

Mitsutoshi Horii is Professor at Shumei University, Japan, and working at Shumei's overseas campus in the United Kingdom, Chaucer College Canterbury. His most recent research focuses on the categories of 'religion' and 'secular' in Euro-American social theories. He also studies the same categories in the Japanese context. In this area, his publication includes the monograph *The Category of Religion in Contemporary Japan: Shūkyō and Temple Buddhism* (London: Palgrave Macmillan, 2018).

Carolina Ivanescu has a background in anthropology, comparative social science and religious studies. She has conducted fieldwork in Tibetan refugee communities and has worked as a volunteer for Tibet support associations in India and abroad. Along her long-term interest in Asian studies and Buddhism she works on themes exploring the construction of tradition and the place of innovation as connected to the religious identity of marginal groups in European modern societies. Carolina is at present lecturer at the Department of History, European Studies and Religious Studies of the University of Amsterdam.

Alison Jasper is a senior lecturer in Religion and Gender at the University of Stirling in Scotland. Recent Publications include: "Reflections on Reading the Bible: Flesh to Female Genius" in Yvonne Sherwood & Anna Fisk (eds), *The Bible and Feminism: Remapping the Field* (Oxford: Oxford University Press, 2017); "Collaborations and Renegotiations: Re-examining the 'Sacred' in the Film-Making of David Gulpilil and Rolf de Heer," *Literature and Theology* 31, no. 2 (2017): 187-199; with John I'Anson, *Schooling Indifference: Reimagining RE in Multi-cultural and Gendered Spaces (Gender, Theology and Spirituality)*, (London & New York: Routledge, 2017).

Michael Marten is a mission historian, political scientist, theologian, and activist. He has studied and taught in several European universities as well as working in the NGO and charity sector in both the Middle East and the UK. He has published widely on Scottish missionaries in the Middle East, as well as on a number of other topics. He is one of the four founder members of the Critical Religion Association, and edited the CRA's online publications for the first four years. He has now left full-time academia and is involved in secondary-level education, whilst continuing to research and write about European involvement in the Middle East, with several articles and a book expected to be published in the near future. His own website is at www.marten.org.uk.

Paige Medlock earned her practice-based PhD in Visual Culture at University of Stirling, Scotland, MLiTT in Visual Culture at University of Aberdeen, MAWME in World Missions at Asbury Theological Seminary, and her BA in Art Education with an emphasis in stained glass, at Asbury University. She teaches, writes, speaks, and creates at the intersection of visual art, education, theology, and culture. She often collaborates with her dad (Professor Emeritus Rudy Medlock, Asbury University), creating stained glass commissioned installations, and some of their work can be seen in Kentucky, Scotland, and the Dominican Republic. Her research explores how art can be a place where an internal shift occurs that enables us to *see* things differently, with care or compassion that leads to action, and she uses the Greek word 'eiden' to distinguish this type of sight. She teaches at Middle Tennessee State University in the department of Art and Design, and has a son named Luke.

Cameron Montgomery is a professor of Canadian Identity and Multiculturalism at Algonquin College in Canada. She completed her doctorate with Naomi Goldenberg at the University of Ottawa in 2017. Cameron owns an art gallery and indie press in Pembroke, Ontario, called Studio Dreamshare. She has produced a number of films long and short, including a documentary for the Canadian Red Cross about Syrian refugee settlement in Canada and two epic fantasy films for children. She has written two speculative fiction novels called *A World So Small* and *Mercury's Crossing* under the pen name Cameron Dreamshare.

Rajalakshmi Nadadur Kannan is a Project Assistant Professor for academic writing at the Center for Global Communication Strategies at University of Tokyo. She received a PhD from University of Stirling, U.K. in 2014. Her dissertation focused on early 20th century South India where performance arts served a religious, gendered nationalistic tool, and its historical implications on contemporary laws on intellectual property rights. Since then, she has been publishing articles on gender, performance arts, and religion. Her current research project looks at nationalism and creation of myths and gendered identities through story-telling. She has taught courses on religion, gender, and postcolonialism in the U.K., journalism in the U.S., and academic writing in English in Thailand. She is also an affiliated researcher at the Centre for the Study of Religion and Culture in Asia at University of Groningen.

Brian Nail is a Professor of English at Florida State College at Jacksonville. He completed his PhD in Literature, Theology, and the Arts at the University of Glasgow, UK. He was awarded an AFR-Marie Curie Cofund grant to conduct postdoctoral research in the Legal Philosophy Research Unit at the University of Luxembourg from 2013-15. In addition to publishing on deconstructive approaches to religious artistic representation, theory of sacrifice, and neoliberalism, he has co-edited and contributed to *Law's Sacrifice: Approaching the Problem of Sacrifice in Law, Literature, and Philosophy* (Routledge, 2019). Through his research and teaching, he seeks to uncover literary, philosophical, and anthropological resources for pursuing social justice and political mutuality in age of austerity. Currently, he is working on a monograph about the sacrificial legacy of settler-colonialism and the dynamics of neoliberal subjectivity in works of twentieth century American literature.

Katja Neumann is a graduate from the University of Stirling. She completed a PhD in Literature and Theology (2014) with a primary focus on the works of German poet-theologian Dorothee Sölle (1929-2003). She examined the relationship between poetic images of motherhood, sisterhood and lovers found in Sölle's poetry and her theological understanding of prayerful expressions of faith in a Christian God. Translating her poetry, which formed a substantial part of her work and remains unpublished, has drawn her attention to the boundaries of linguistic self-assertions on gendered experiences. She sustains a continued wider interest in women's responses around issues of gender and sexuality in society, faith and in writing. Five years on from graduation, she is working as administrator for the Scottish Prison Service (SPS) and is part of the Equality and Diversity ambassadors at the SPS.

Per-Erik Nilsson is Associate Professor in Sociology of Religion and Director at the Center for Multidisciplinary Studies of Racism (CEMFOR), Uppsala University. Nilsson has published extensively on the intersections of secularism, religion, and politics. His latest book is *French Populism and Discourses on Secularism* (New York and London: Bloomsbury, 2018).

Francis Stewart is the Director of the Edward Bailey Research Centre and Implicit Religion Research Fellow at Bishop Grosseteste University, Lincoln. She is the author *of Punk Rock is my Religion: Straight Edge Punk and 'Religious' Identity*(2017, Routledge) alongside journal articles on the connections between aspects of punk rock and the creation and use of the categories of 'religion', 'secular', 'sacred' and 'profane'. Her current work is focused on marginalization within punk memorialization and curation, with an emphasis on sound capture and the role museums' understand and display of 'religion' has had on creating and maintaining that marginalization. Her most recent publication on her current work is "No More Heroes Anymore": Marginalization in Punk Narration and Curation. Journal of Punk & Post Punk, Vol. 8.2 pp 209- 226.

www.ingramcontent.com/pod-product-compliance
Lightning Source LLC
Chambersburg PA
CBHW030908080526
44589CB00010B/208